Contents

Nutrition experts tell us

to cut back on sugary, fatty, and salty foods, but snacking by itself isn't bad. In fact...

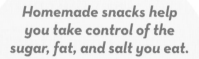

Snacks are fantastic! They can:

- Help keep your **blood sugar steady**
- **Satisfy your appetite** between meals
- **Give you a boost** before a workout— or help your body recover afterwards
- Help you get all the **healthy nutrition** your body needs

Homemade snacks help you take control of the sugar, fat, and salt you eat.

- These snacks give you **more variety** over the foods you find in convenience stores and vending machines.
- Plus, they'll help you eat **more produce** and whole grains.

Snacktastic *will make your day better!*

- Every snack is **150 calories or fewer**
- **At-a-glance nutrition info** shows you protein, fat, carbs, and fiber

COLORFUL TAGS
help you find the perfect snack!

DAIRY FREE ▶ *These snacks have no milk, cheese, yogurt, or other dairy products.*

ENERGY SUSTAINING ▶ *Keep your energy on an even keel with these snacks. They have a combination of fiber, protein, and complex carbs to promote the slow release of glucose into the bloodstream.*

GLUTEN FREE ▶ *Choose these snacks if you need to avoid gluten, the proteins found in wheat.*

HIGH PROTEIN ▶ *These snacks contain at least 25% of their calories from protein.*

LOW-CARB ▶ *If you're counting carbs, grab these snacks with 10% or fewer calories coming from carbohydrates.*

PRE-WORKOUT ▶ *Fuel up for exercise with these snacks. At least 40% of the calories come from carbs that are easy to digest. They're also low in fiber, low in fat, and low to moderate in protein.*

POST-WORKOUT ▶ *These post-workout snacks contain at least 40% of their calories from carbs to replenish your glycogen stores, and at least 15% of their calories from protein to help your muscles mend after exercise.*

bonus!
Can't get to a kitchen? Check out the **Great Packaged Snacks** (page 214).

snack smart!
Every recipe is **150 calories or fewer** per serving and keeps saturated fat and sodium in check.

plus...
Use **Make It a Meal** suggestions to pair snacks together for a satisfying breakfast, lunch, or dinner

st●ck up wisely

Keep these ingredients on hand so you're always ready for a creamy, crunchy, sweet, or savory snack.

creamy!

avocados
heart-healthy fats
+ (surprise!) fiber

bananas
loaded with
potassium, which
is great for your
heart and muscles

**cheeses, milk,
yogurt** bone-
building calcium

canned beans
low in fat, high in fiber

nut butters
filling fiber + protein

tofu
a secret protein-
packed ingredient

crunchy!

nuts
protein + healthy fats

popcorn
lots of antioxidants

oatmeal fiber

**breads, pita,
tortillas** go whole
grain for fiber and
vitamins

**canned chick-
peas** appetite-
satisfying fiber

crunchy veggies
vitamins + minerals

sweet!

cereals
choose whole
grain

dried fruit
more antioxidant
power than fresh fruit

cocoa
delivers chocolate
flavor without
the fat

**honey + maple
syrup** natural
sweeteners that blend
well in liquid

jams + preserves
use all-natural or low-
sugar for fruit flavor
without a lot of sugar

fresh fruit
fiber, antioxidants +
a little hydration, too

savory!

cheese
calcium + protein

pesto
heart-healthy fats

tapenades
heart-healthy fats

**whole-grain
chips** go whole
grain for more of
vitamins B and E

herbs
low-cal flavor

lemons + limes
a squeeze adds
vitamin C and
potassium

mustard
lots of low-fat zing

phyllo shells
quick, low-cal

CREAMY

Dips, smoothies, parfaits, and spreads

smooth!

luscious!

mmm!

carbs: 23g ■ fat: 0.3g
fiber: 2g ■ protein: 9.7g

Vanilla-Berry Smoothies

1 (5.3-ounce) carton vanilla fat-free Greek yogurt
1 cup frozen mixed berries
½ cup fat-free milk
2 teaspoons honey
3 ice cubes

1. Place first 4 ingredients in a blender; process until smooth. Remove center cap from blender lid; with blender on, add ice cubes, 1 at a time, processing until smooth. Serves 2 (serving size: about 1 cup)

CALORIES 120; **FAT** 0.3g (sat 0.0g, mono 0.1g, poly 0.2g); **PROTEIN** 9.7g; **CARB** 23g; **FIBER** 2g; **CHOL** 1mg; **IRON** 0.2mg; **SODIUM** 59mg; **CALC** 87mg

---

MAKE IT A MEAL *(see page 218 for complete nutrition)*

| 1 serving Vanilla-Berry Smoothies |  | 2 sheets graham crackers | | 2 tablespoons peanut butter |

---

total time
3 min.

Use a 6-ounce container of vanilla low-fat yogurt if you want a sweeter smoothie.

GLUTEN FREE

HIGH PROTEIN

POST-WORKOUT

ENERGY SUSTAINING

carbs: 17.8g ▪ fat: 0.3g ▪ fiber: 1.4g ▪ protein: 10.9g

Blueberry-Yogurt Parfaits

1 cup plain fat-free Greek yogurt
¼ teaspoon grated lemon rind
2 teaspoons honey
½ cup blueberries
2 tablespoons multigrain cluster cereal

1. Combine first 3 ingredients in a small bowl. Spoon 2 tablespoons yogurt mixture into each of 2 parfait glasses. Top each with 2 tablespoons blueberries. Repeat layers. Top each serving with 1 tablespoon cereal. Serve immediately. Serves 2 (serving size: 1 parfait)

CALORIES 115; **FAT** 0.3g (sat 0g, mono 0.1g, poly 0.1g); **PROTEIN** 10.9g; **CARB** 17.8g; **FIBER** 1.4g; **CHOL** 0mg; **IRON** 0.2mg; **SODIUM** 56mg; **CALC** 81mg

total time
5 min.

Layer the berries and yogurt ahead, and store in the refrigerator. Top with cereal just before serving.

HIGH PROTEIN

POST-WORKOUT

carbs: 22.7g ▪ fat: 1.1g
fiber: 3.3g ▪ protein: 7.6g

Banana-Blueberry Smoothies

1 cup frozen blueberries
½ cup silken tofu
2 tablespoons water
1 teaspoon vanilla extract
1½ medium-sized ripe bananas, broken into pieces
1 (5.3-ounce) container plain fat-free Greek yogurt

1. Place all ingredients in a blender; process until smooth, scraping sides as necessary. Serves 3 (serving size: 1 cup)

CALORIES 132; **FAT** 1.1g (sat 0g, mono 0.3g, poly 0.5g); **PROTEIN** 7.6g; **CARB** 22.7g; **FIBER** 3.3g; **CHOL** 0mg; **IRON** 0.5mg; **SODIUM** 23mg; **CALC** 92mg

total time
5 min.

These protein-packed smoothies are sure to keep you satisfied all morning.

GLUTEN FREE

POST-WORKOUT

ENERGY SUSTAINING

carbs: 14g ▪ **fat:** 3.3g ▪ **fiber:** 1.9g ▪ **protein:** 2.6g

Butternut Squash Spread with Pepitas

1½ cups (½-inch) cubed peeled butternut squash (about 1 pound)

Cooking spray

1 teaspoon olive oil

½ cup diced onion

1½ teaspoons chopped fresh sage

¼ teaspoon salt

⅛ teaspoon freshly ground black pepper

2 garlic cloves, minced

Dash of crushed red pepper

¼ cup chopped sun-dried tomatoes, packed without oil

2 tablespoons unsalted pumpkinseed kernels, toasted

40 toasted garlic bagel chips

total time
40 min.

Add a little water when pureeing the squash to achieve a creamy consistency, if necessary.

DAIRY FREE

1. Place butternut squash in a medium saucepan; cover with water 2 inches above squash. Bring to a boil; cover, reduce heat, and cook 15 minutes or until tender. Drain.

2. Heat a large nonstick skillet over medium-high heat. Coat pan with cooking spray. Add oil to pan; swirl to coat. Add onion to pan; sauté 4 minutes or until tender. Add sage and next 4 ingredients (through red pepper); sauté 2 minutes. Cool.

3. Place squash, onion mixture, and sun-dried tomatoes in a food processor; process until smooth. Spoon into a medium bowl; sprinkle with pumpkinseed kernels. Serve with bagel chips. Serves 8 (serving size: 3 tablespoons spread and 5 chips)

CALORIES 96; **FAT** 3.3g (sat 0.5g, mono 0.8g, poly 0.5g); **PROTEIN** 2.6g; **CARB** 14g; **FIBER** 1.9g; **CHOL** 0mg; **IRON** 1.2mg; **SODIUM** 186mg; **CALC** 23mg

carbs: 19.4g ▪ **fat:** 4.3g
fiber: 5g ▪ **protein:** 6.4g

Curried Hummus

2 (15-ounce) cans no-salt-
   added chickpeas
   (garbanzo beans), drained
2 tablespoons water
2 tablespoons extra-virgin
   olive oil

1 tablespoon fresh lemon
   juice
2 teaspoons curry powder
½ teaspoon salt
4 cups broccoli florets

1. Place first 6 ingredients in a food processor; process until smooth. Serve with broccoli florets. Serves 8 (serving size: ⅓ cup hummus and ½ cup broccoli florets)

CALORIES 139; **FAT** 4.3g (sat 0.5g, mono 2.5g, poly 0.4g); **PROTEIN** 6.4g; **CARB** 19.4g; **FIBER** 5g; **CHOL** 0mg; **IRON** 1.5mg; **SODIUM** 169mg; **CALC** 58mg

total time
4 min.

Hummus, a Mediterranean classic, gets an Indian twist with curry powder.

DAIRY FREE

GLUTEN FREE

POST-WORKOUT

ENERGY SUSTAINING

carbs: 4.1g ■ fat: 9.8g ■ protein: 3g
fiber: 1.4g

Curried Yogurt Dip

½ cup plain 2% reduced-fat Greek yogurt
½ cup canola mayonnaise
1½ tablespoons chopped fresh cilantro
1 tablespoon fresh lime juice
1½ teaspoons hot curry powder
1 garlic clove, minced
8 celery sticks, cut in half

1. Combine first 6 ingredients in a small bowl. Serve with celery sticks. Serves 4 (serving size: ¼ cup dip and 4 pieces of celery)

CALORIES 124; **FAT** 9.8g (sat 0.5g, mono 5.2g, poly 3.1g); **PROTEIN** 3g; **CARB** 4.1g; **FIBER** 1.4g; **CHOL** 2mg; **IRON** 0.4mg; **SODIUM** 198mg; **CALC** 26mg

---

MAKE IT A MEAL *(see page 218 for complete nutrition)*

2 servings Curried Yogurt Dip served with celery in recipe	➕	1 serving Crispy Spiced Chickpeas, page 69

total time
5 min.

Pair this spicy dip with an assortment of vegetables, using whatever fresh seasonal produce you have on hand.

GLUTEN FREE

LOW-CARB

carbs: 6.8g ▪ fat: 2.3g
fiber: 0.8g ▪ protein: 4.5g

Feta-Mint Dip

1 cup plain 2% reduced-fat Greek yogurt
½ cup (2 ounces) crumbled feta cheese
½ cup finely chopped English cucumber
3 tablespoons chopped fresh mint
2 tablespoons sliced green onions
¼ teaspoon freshly ground black pepper
¼ teaspoon grated lemon rind
⅛ teaspoon salt
Freshly ground black pepper (optional)
8 mini whole-wheat pitas, cut into 4 wedges each

total time
7 min.

Make this dip the day before, and refrigerate it overnight to allow the yogurt to fully absorb all the flavors.

POST-WORKOUT

1. Place yogurt and feta in a food processor; process until smooth. Transfer to a small bowl. Stir in cucumber and next 5 ingredients (through salt). Sprinkle with additional black pepper, if desired. Serve with pita breads. Serves 8 (serving size: about 3½ tablespoons dip and 4 pita pieces)

CALORIES 66; **FAT** 2.3g (sat 1.4g, mono 0.9g, poly 0.1g); **PROTEIN** 4.5g; **CARB** 6.8g; **FIBER** 0.8g; **CHOL** 8mg; **IRON** 0.4mg; **SODIUM** 172mg; **CALC** 66mg

---

MAKE IT A MEAL *(see page 218 for complete nutrition)*

| 2 servings Feta-Mint Dip served with pita bread wedges in recipe | | 2 servings Toasted Cashew Hummus served with cucumbers in recipe, page 51 |

---

carbs: 6g ▪ **fat:** 3.4g
fiber: 0.4g ▪ **protein:** 1.9g

Fig-Goat Cheese Spread

1 (8-ounce) package ⅓-less-fat cream cheese, softened
⅓ cup (2.65 ounces) goat cheese
¼ cup fig preserves
¼ cup chopped dried figs
1 teaspoon grated lemon rind
2 teaspoons fresh lemon juice
¼ cup chopped walnuts, toasted
60 nut and rice crackers

1. Combine first 7 ingredients in large bowl, stirring until blended. Serve with crackers. Serves 30 (serving size: 1 tablespoon spread and 2 crackers)

CALORIES 62; **FAT** 3.4g (sat 1.5g, mono 0.8g, poly 0.5g); **PROTEIN** 1.9g; **CARB** 6g; **FIBER** 0.4g; **CHOL** 8mg; **IRON** 0.2mg; **SODIUM** 54mg; **CALC** 20mg

total time
10 min.

Serve this spread at room temperature with pita chips or apple slices.

GLUTEN FREE

carbs: 4.3g ∎ fat: 5.6g
fiber: 0.8g ∎ protein: 1.2g

Fresh Herb Dip

1 (16-ounce) carton reduced-fat sour cream
1 cup light mayonnaise
2 garlic cloves, pressed
3 tablespoons chopped fresh parsley
3 tablespoons chopped fresh dill
¼ teaspoon kosher salt
¼ teaspoon freshly ground black pepper
48 baby carrots
1 large cucumber, cut into thin slices

total time
8 min.

Chopped mint would make a nice addition to this herb dip.

GLUTEN FREE

LOW-CARB

1. Combine first 7 ingredients in a bowl, stirring until well blended. Serve immediately, or cover and chill until ready to serve. Serve with baby carrots and cucumber slices. Serves 24 (serving size: 2 tablespoons dip, 2 baby carrots, and 2 cucumber slices)

CALORIES 72; **FAT** 5.6g (sat 2.0g, mono 0.8g, poly 1.8g); **PROTEIN** 1.2g; **CARB** 4.3g; **FIBER** 0.8g; **CHOL** 13mg; **IRON** 0.3mg; **SODIUM** 115mg; **CALC** 43mg

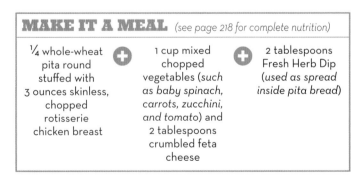

MAKE IT A MEAL (see page 218 for complete nutrition)

¼ whole-wheat pita round stuffed with 3 ounces skinless, chopped rotisserie chicken breast ➕ 1 cup mixed chopped vegetables (such as baby spinach, carrots, zucchini, and tomato) and 2 tablespoons crumbled feta cheese ➕ 2 tablespoons Fresh Herb Dip (used as spread inside pita bread)

carbs: 0.8g ▪ **fat:** 2.1g ▪ **fiber:** 0g ▪ **protein:** 0.7g

Roasted Garlic-
Cream Cheese Balls

1 (8-ounce) block ⅓-less-fat cream cheese, softened
2 teaspoons bottled minced roasted garlic
¼ teaspoon ground cumin
⅛ teaspoon crushed red pepper
⅛ teaspoon freshly ground black pepper
6 tablespoons chopped fresh cilantro

Spread this garlicky goodness on apple slices, flatbread crackers, or toasted baguette slices.

GLUTEN FREE

LOW-CARB

1. Combine first 5 ingredients in a small bowl, stirring until well blended.

2. Shape mixture into 24 (½-inch) balls. Place cilantro in a shallow dish. Roll each ball in cilantro. Chill until ready to serve. Serves 24 (serving size: 1 ball)

CALORIES 25; **FAT** 2.1g (sat 1.4g, mono 0.5g, poly 0.1g); **PROTEIN** 0.7g; **CARB** 0.8g; **FIBER** 0g; **CHOL** 7mg; **IRON** 0mg; **SODIUM** 37mg; **CALC** 7mg

---

MAKE IT A MEAL *(see page 218 for complete nutrition)*

| 1½ cups tomato and basil soup | ➕ | 2 servings Roasted Garlic–Cream Cheese Balls | ➕ | 6 whole-grain crackers |

carbs: 31.9g ▪ fat: 0.7g
fiber: 2.9g ▪ protein: 6.3g

Go-Getter Green Smoothies

1 cup (½-inch) cubes honeydew melon
1 cup bagged fresh baby spinach
1 cup sliced ripe banana, frozen (about 1 large)
½ cup vanilla light soy milk
1 (5.3-ounce) container fat-free Greek yogurt with honey
1 cubed peeled kiwifruit

1. Place all ingredients in a blender. Process until smooth. Serve immediately. Serves 2 (serving size: 1 cup)

CALORIES 149; **FAT** 0.7g (sat 0.1g, mono 0.1g, poly 0.3g); **PROTEIN** 6.3g; **CARB** 31.9g; **FIBER** 2.9g; **CHOL** 0mg; **IRON** 0.7mg; **SODIUM** 61mg; **CALC** 120mg

total time
5 min.

Be sure to try this smoothie in the summer when ripe, sweet honeydew melon is available.

GLUTEN FREE

POST-WORKOUT

ENERGY SUSTAINING

carbs: 13.6g ■ fat: 4.5g
fiber: 1.5g ■ protein: 3.9g

Jalapeño-Corn Dip and Corn Chips

Cooking spray
2½ cups fresh corn kernels (about 4 ears)
3 tablespoons finely chopped seeded jalapeño pepper
3 ounces reduced-fat extra-sharp cheddar cheese, shredded
½ cup fat-free mayonnaise
¼ cup chopped green onions
1 (8-ounce) carton reduced-fat sour cream
1 (4-ounce) can chopped green chiles, drained
Chopped fresh cilantro (optional)
70 baked corn tortilla chips

1. Heat a medium nonstick skillet over medium-high heat. Coat pan with cooking spray. Add corn kernels and jalapeño; sauté 6 minutes or just until tender. Remove from heat; stir in cheese and next 4 ingredients (through chiles). Serve warm. Garnish with cilantro, if desired. Serve with tortilla chips. Serves 14 (serving size: ¼ cup dip and 5 chips)

CALORIES 105; **FAT** 4.5g (sat 2.2g, mono 1.3g, poly 0.3g); **PROTEIN** 3.9g; **CARB** 13.6g; **FIBER** 1.5g; **CHOL** 13mg; **IRON** 0.3mg; **SODIUM** 199mg; **CALC** 92mg

carbs: 13g ■ fat: 5.5g
fiber: 3.4g ■ protein: 4.4g

◀ Artichoke Spread

1 (10-ounce) package frozen artichoke hearts, thawed and chopped
2 tablespoons chopped fresh flat-leaf parsley
6 ounces ⅓-less-fat cream cheese, softened
2 tablespoons fresh lemon juice
¼ teaspoon freshly ground black pepper
Spicy Pita Crisps

1. Combine first 5 ingredients. Serve with Spicy Pita Crisps. Serves 8 (serving size: 2 tablespoons spread and 4 crisps)

CALORIES 116; **FAT** 5.5g (sat 2.8g, mono 1.3g, poly 0.5g); **PROTEIN** 4.4g; **CARB** 13g; **FIBER** 3.4g; **CHOL** 16mg; **IRON** 0.8mg; **SODIUM** 210mg; **CALC** 47mg

total time
15 min.

This tangy spread gets a kick from cumin-dusted pita crisps. Make it while the pita crisps bake.

POST-WORKOUT
ENERGY SUSTAINING

◀ Spicy Pita Crisps

2 (6-inch) whole-wheat pitas
Olive oil–flavored cooking spray
½ teaspoon ground cumin
¼ teaspoon freshly ground black pepper
⅛ teaspoon kosher salt
⅛ teaspoon ground red pepper

1. Preheat oven to 425°.

2. Cut each pita into 8 wedges. Split each wedge in half. Place in single layer on a baking sheet coated with cooking spray. Combine cumin and next 3 ingredients. Sprinkle evenly over pita wedges. Lightly coat pita wedges with cooking spray.

3. Bake at 425° for 5 minutes or until browned and crisp. Serves 8 (serving size: 4 crisps)

CALORIES 43; **FAT** 0.5g (sat 0.1g, mono 0.1g, poly 0.2g); **PROTEIN** 1.6g; **CARB** 8.9g; **FIBER** 1.3g; **CHOL** 0mg; **IRON** 0.5g; **SODIUM** 115mg; **CALC** 4mg

carbs: 9.4g ▪ fat: 1.7g ▪ fiber: 3g ▪ protein: 2.1g

Lemon, Mint, and White Bean Dip

- 1 garlic clove
- 1 (15-ounce) can no-salt-added cannellini beans, rinsed and drained
- 2 tablespoons chopped fresh mint
- 1 teaspoon grated lemon rind
- 1½ tablespoons fresh lemon juice
- 1 tablespoon extra-virgin olive oil
- ¼ teaspoon salt
- ¼ teaspoon freshly ground black pepper
- 50 baby carrots

total time
5 min.

You can make this dip in advance, and store in an air-tight container in the refrigerator up to 1 week.

DAIRY FREE

GLUTEN FREE

1. Drop garlic through food chute with processor on; process until minced. Add beans and next 6 ingredients (through pepper); process until smooth. Cover and chill until ready to serve. Serve with carrots. Serves 10 (serving size: 2 tablespoons dip and 5 baby carrots)

CALORIES 60; **FAT** 1.7g (sat 0.2g, mono 1.0g, poly 0.2g); **PROTEIN** 2.1g; **CARB** 9.4g; **FIBER** 3g; **CHOL** 0mg; **IRON** 1.0mg; **SODIUM** 104mg; **CALC** 29mg

MAKE IT A MEAL (see page 218 for complete nutrition)

| 2 servings Lemon, Mint, and White Bean Dip served with baby carrots in recipe | ➕ | 2 servings Feta Pita Crisps, page 77 | ➕ | 1 Frozen Peanut Butter–Banana Pop, page 127 |

carbs: _20.3g_ ▪ fat: _2.1g_ ▪ fiber: _1.5g_ ▪ protein: _1.8g_

Lemony Fruit Dip

¼ cup sugar, divided
1 large egg
2½ tablespoons fresh lemon juice
¼ cup water
1½ teaspoons cornstarch
½ teaspoon vanilla extract

1½ cups frozen reduced-calorie whipped topping, thawed
Lemon rind (optional)
Fresh mint leaves (optional)
42 strawberries

total time
37 min.

Serve with fresh fruit such as strawberries, pineapple, or apple.

GLUTEN FREE

PRE-WORKOUT

1. Combine 2 tablespoons sugar, egg, and lemon juice in a small bowl; stir well with a whisk.

2. Combine 2 tablespoons sugar, ¼ cup water, and cornstarch in a small saucepan; bring to a boil. Cook 30 seconds or until thickened, stirring constantly. Remove from heat. Slowly pour beaten egg mixture into water mixture, stirring constantly. Cook over medium heat 2 minutes or until thick, stirring constantly. Remove from heat; stir in vanilla. Cool completely. Fold in whipped topping. Garnish with lemon rind and fresh mint, if desired. Serve with strawberries. Serves 7 (serving size: about ¼ cup dip and 6 strawberries)

CALORIES 116; **FAT** 2.1g (sat 1.9g, mono 0.1g, poly 0.1g); **PROTEIN** 1.8g; **CARB** 20.3g; **FIBER** 1.5g; **CHOL** 30mg; **IRON** 0.5mg; **SODIUM** 14mg; **CALC** 19mg

carbs: 13g ▪ fat: 5.4g ▪ fiber: 2.1g ▪ protein: 3.3g

◀ Peanut Butter–Banana Dip

½ cup chunky peanut butter
⅓ cup mashed ripe banana
1 tablespoon honey
¼ teaspoon ground cinnamon
1 (6-ounce) carton vanilla fat-free organic yogurt
3 apples, each cut into 12 slices

1. Combine first 5 ingredients. Serve with apple slices. Serves 12 (serving size: 2 tablespoons dip and 3 apple slices)

CALORIES 106; **FAT** 5.4g (sat 0.9g, mono 2.6g, poly 1.6g); **PROTEIN** 3.3g; **CARB** 13g; **FIBER** 2.1g; **CHOL** 0mg; **IRON** 0.3mg; **SODIUM** 60mg; **CALC** 24mg

total time
4 min.

Serve this protein-packed dip with apple slices, crackers, or pretzels for an afternoon snack.

GLUTEN FREE

Navy Bean Dip

1 (16-ounce) can navy beans, rinsed and drained
⅓ cup plain fat-free yogurt
1 garlic clove, halved
2 teaspoons red wine vinegar
1 ounce sun-dried tomatoes, packed without oil, finely chopped (about 8)
¼ cup pitted kalamata olives, finely chopped
42 table water crackers

1. Place first 4 ingredients in a food processor; process until smooth. Place bean mixture in a serving bowl. Combine sun-dried tomatoes and olives; sprinkle over bean mixture. Serve with crackers. Serves 14 (serving size: 2 tablespoons dip and 3 crackers)

CALORIES 92; **FAT** 1.7g (sat 0.4g, mono 0.5g, poly 0.2g); **PROTEIN** 4.2g; **CARB** 15.9g; **FIBER** 2.2g; **CHOL** 0mg; **IRON** 0.7mg; **SODIUM** 170mg; **CALC** 31mg

total time
10 min.

Dotted with olives and sun-dried tomatoes, this Mediterranean-inspired snack is swanky enough for a party.

POST-WORKOUT

ENERGY SUSTAINING

carbs: 11.3g ▪ fat: 2.7g ▪ fiber: 2g ▪ protein: 3.6g

Pumpkin-Parmesan Hummus

total time
13 min.

2 large garlic cloves
1 (16-ounce) can reduced-sodium chickpeas (garbanzo beans), rinsed and drained
1 cup canned pumpkin
½ cup (2 ounces) freshly shredded Parmigiano-Reggiano cheese
3 tablespoons fresh lime juice
3 tablespoons plain fat-free Greek yogurt
1 teaspoon Southwest chipotle seasoning blend
¼ teaspoon salt
60 pita chips

Pumpkin isn't just for pie; it's a type of squash, and it works in savory recipes, too.

POST-WORKOUT

ENERGY SUSTAINING

1. Drop garlic through food chute of a food processor with processor on. Process until minced. Add chickpeas; process until chopped. Add pumpkin and next 5 ingredients (through salt); process until smooth. Serve with pita chips. Serves 20 (serving size: 2 tablespoons hummus and 3 pita chips)

CALORIES 82; **FAT** 2.7g (sat 0.7g, mono 0.3g, poly 0.1g); **PROTEIN** 3.6g; **CARB** 11.3g; **FIBER** 2g; **CHOL** 2mg; **IRON** 0.8mg; **SODIUM** 172mg; **CALC** 48mg

carbs: 8.1g ▪ fat: 3.5g
fiber: 0.9g ▪ protein: 2.8g

Southwest Spinach Dip

1 (10-ounce) package frozen chopped spinach
1 (10-ounce) can diced tomatoes and green chiles, undrained
1 cup (4 ounces) pre-shredded reduced-fat 4-cheese Mexican blend cheese
6 ounces (¾ cup) ⅓-less-fat cream cheese
Cooking spray
120 baked tortilla chip scoops

1. Preheat oven to 400°.

2. Place frozen spinach in a colander; rinse with hot water until thawed. Drain, pressing until barely moist.

3. Combine spinach, tomatoes, and cheeses in a large bowl. Spoon spinach mixture into an 11 x 7-inch baking dish coated with cooking spray. Bake at 400° for 23 minutes or until lightly browned and bubbly. Serve with tortilla chip scoops. Serves 24 (serving size: 2 tablespoons dip and 5 scoops)

CALORIES 75; **FAT** 3.5g (sat 1.7g, mono 0.4g, poly 0.1g); **PROTEIN** 2.8g; **CARB** 8.1g; **FIBER** 0.9g; **CHOL** 8mg; **IRON** 0.4mg; **SODIUM** 124mg; **CALC** 94mg

total time
28 min.

Be sure to squeeze as much liquid from the spinach as possible to avoid a watery dip.

GLUTEN FREE
POST-WORKOUT

carbs: 15.3g ▪ fat: 5.7g
fiber: 2.8g ▪ protein: 3g

Roasted Vegetable Dip

1 pound carrots, cut into ½-inch slices
1 large Vidalia or other sweet onion, cut into 6 wedges
1 red bell pepper, cut into 1-inch pieces
1 tablespoon olive oil
2 tablespoons chili sauce with garlic
¼ cup tahini (roasted sesame seed paste)
¼ teaspoon salt
¼ teaspoon pepper
Fresh flat-leaf parsley, chopped (optional)
9 sesame breadsticks

1. Preheat oven to 450°.

2. Combine first 4 ingredients in a large bowl, and toss well. Place vegetables on a jelly-roll pan. Bake at 450° for 35 minutes or until tender, stirring every 15 minutes.

3. Place roasted vegetables, chili sauce, tahini, salt, and pepper in a food processor; process until smooth. Garnish with chopped parsley, if desired. Serve with breadsticks. Serves 9 (serving size: ¼ cup dip and 1 breadstick)

CALORIES 116; **FAT** 5.7g (sat 1.0g, mono 2.4g, poly 1.8g); **PROTEIN** 3g; **CARB** 15.3g; **FIBER** 2.8g; **CHOL** 0mg; **IRON** 0.7mg; **SODIUM** 177mg; **CALC** 41mg

total time
43 min.

You can find tahini in supermarkets or in Middle Eastern food stores.

DAIRY FREE

carbs: 11.6g ▪ fat: 6.6g
fiber: 1.9g ▪ protein: 4.8g

Lemon-Spinach Dip with Walnuts

1 (10-ounce) package frozen chopped spinach, thawed, drained, and squeezed dry
¾ cup plain 2% reduced-fat Greek yogurt
1 teaspoon freshly ground black pepper
1 teaspoon bottled minced garlic
1 teaspoon grated lemon rind
½ teaspoon salt
¼ cup chopped walnuts, toasted
Grated lemon rind (optional)
70 baked unsalted sweet potato chips

1. Combine first 6 ingredients in a medium bowl. Cover and chill until ready to serve. Sprinkle with walnuts and lemon rind, if desired, just before serving. Serve with sweet potato chips. Serves 7 (serving size: 3 tablespoons dip and 10 chips)

CALORIES 121; **FAT** 6.6g (sat 1.0g, mono 0.7g, poly 1.6g); **PROTEIN** 4.8g; **CARB** 11.6g; **FIBER** 1.9g; **CHOL** 2mg; **IRON** 1.1mg; **SODIUM** 37mg; **CALC** 73mg

---

MAKE IT A MEAL (see page 218 for complete nutrition)

| 2 servings Lemon-Spinach Dip with Walnuts served with sweet potato chips in recipe | ➕ | 1 serving Roasted Edamame, page 211 |

total time
8 min.

This cold spinach dip is a refreshing twist on the traditional baked version. Serve with pita chips or vegetable chips.

GLUTEN FREE

carbs: 8.2g ▪ fat: 5.7g
fiber: 1.5g ▪ protein: 2.7g

Toasted Cashew Hummus

total time
13 min.

Toasting the roasted cashews deepens their flavor.

DAIRY FREE

GLUTEN FREE

1 cup jumbo cashews, roasted in sea salt
2 garlic cloves
¾ cup water
¼ cup tahini (roasted sesame seed paste)
2 tablespoons fresh lime juice
1 tablespoon olive oil
1 teaspoon ground cumin
¼ teaspoon salt
1 (15.5-ounce) can chickpeas (garbanzo beans), rinsed and drained
2 teaspoons chopped fresh cilantro (optional)
2 large cucumbers, cut into thin slices

1. Preheat oven to 350°.

2. Spread cashews in a shallow pan. Bake at 350° for 7 minutes, stirring occasionally.

3. Drop garlic through food chute with food processor on; process until minced. Add cashews, ¾ cup water, and next 6 ingredients (through chickpeas); process until smooth. Garnish with cilantro, if desired. Serve with cucumbers. Serves 20 (serving size: 2 tablespoons hummus and 4 cucumber slices)

CALORIES 91; **FAT** 5.7g (sat 1.0g, mono 3.0g, poly 1.4g); **PROTEIN** 2.7g; **CARB** 8.2g; **FIBER** 1.5g; **CHOL** 0mg; **IRON** 0.9mg; **SODIUM** 104mg; **CALC** 19mg

carbs: 13.6g ▪ fat: 5.4g
fiber: 3.4g ▪ protein: 2.1g

Tomato-Avocado Dip

1 cup chopped tomato
1½ teaspoons chopped fresh cilantro
1 tablespoon fresh lime juice
¼ teaspoon salt
¼ teaspoon ground cumin
1 ripe peeled avocado, coarsely mashed
1 garlic clove, minced
36 baked tortilla chips

1. Combine first 7 ingredients in a medium bowl. Serve immediately with chips. Serves 6 (serving size: ¼ cup dip and 6 tortilla chips)

CALORIES 103; **FAT** 5.4g (sat 0.7g, mono 3.3g, poly 0.6g); **PROTEIN** 2.1g; **CARB** 13.6g; **FIBER** 3.4g; **CHOL** 0mg; **IRON** 0.4mg; **SODIUM** 177mg; **CALC** 24mg

total time
5 min.

This dip's creamy texture makes it an ideal sandwich spread or taco topping, too.

DAIRY FREE

GLUTEN FREE

MAKE IT A MEAL *(see page 218 for complete nutrition)*

| ½ cup canned, drained black beans served over 1 cup cooked brown rice | ➕ | ¼ cup Tomato-Avocado Dip *(served as topping for rice and beans)* | ➕ | 2 tablespoons shredded reduced-fat cheddar cheese |

CRUNCHY

Snack mixes, granolas, nuts, popcorn, and more

munch!

nosh!

crunch!

carbs: 19.9g ▪ fat: 5.4g ▪ fiber: 2.4g ▪ protein: 2.8g

Almond-Apricot Granola

2 cups old-fashioned rolled oats
1 cup sliced almonds
¼ cup honey
2 tablespoons canola oil
¼ teaspoon ground cinnamon
⅛ teaspoon salt
Cooking spray
1 cup dried apricots, coarsely chopped

1. Preheat oven to 300°.

2. Combine oats and almonds in a large bowl. Combine honey and oil in a small saucepan. Bring to a boil, stirring occasionally. Stir in cinnamon and salt; pour honey mixture over oat mixture, tossing until oats are thoroughly coated.

3. Spread oat mixture evenly onto a 17 x 12 x 1-inch pan coated with cooking spray. Bake at 300° for 35 to 38 minutes, stirring every 10 minutes, until granola is golden brown. Let cool on baking sheet. Stir in apricots. Store in an airtight container. Serves 16 (serving size: about ¼ cup)

CALORIES 136; **FAT** 5.4g (sat 0.6g, mono 2.4g, poly 2.2g); **PROTEIN** 2.8g; **CARB** 19.9g; **FIBER** 2.4g; **CHOL** 0mg; **IRON** 1.3mg; **SODIUM** 20mg; **CALC** 22mg

total time
42 min.

Use this granola for a quick topping for oatmeal or yogurt, or for an on-the-go breakfast all by itself.

`DAIRY FREE`

MAKE IT A MEAL (see page 218 for complete nutrition)

| 1 envelope high-fiber maple and brown sugar instant oatmeal | ➕ | 1 serving Almond-Apricot Granola (used as topping for oatmeal) | ➕ | 1 cup fat-free milk |

carbs: 14.6g ■ fat: 2.4g

fiber: 1.2g ■ protein: 3.4g

Cheddar-Apple Cracker Bites

2 (0.7-ounce) slices reduced-fat cheddar cheese, cut into quarters

8 (0.1-ounce, 3 x 1½-inch) flatbread crackers

24 thin vertical Fuji apple slices (1 medium)

1 tablespoon honey

2 teaspoons stone-ground mustard

1. Place 1 cheese quarter on top of each cracker. Top each with 3 apple slices.

2. Combine honey and mustard in a small bowl. Drizzle evenly over apples. Serves 4 (serving size: 2 topped crackers)

CALORIES 90; **FAT** 2.4g (sat 1.2g, mono 0.6g, poly 0.1g); **PROTEIN** 3.4g; **CARB** 14.6g; **FIBER** 1.2g; **CHOL** 8mg; **IRON** 0.4mg; **SODIUM** 156mg; **CALC** 144mg

MAKE IT A MEAL (see page 218 for complete nutrition)		
3 servings Cheddar-Apple Cracker Bites	➕	1 Strawberry-Ginger Yogurt Pop, page 161

total time
5 min.

Using different cheeses or mustards, or even pears instead of apples, gives you more options.

POST-WORKOUT

carbs: 13.8g ■ fat: 4.2g
fiber: 3g ■ protein: 3.2g

Cherry-Orange Granola **with Coconut**

⅓ cup slivered almonds
¼ cup chopped pecans
2½ cups protein and high-fiber crunch cereal
¼ cup flaked sweetened coconut

1½ teaspoons grated orange rind
½ cup dried cherries

1. Heat a large nonstick skillet over medium-high heat. Add almonds and pecans; cook 4 minutes or until toasted, stirring frequently. Pour nuts into a large bowl.

2. Add cereal to pan. Sprinkle cereal with coconut; cook 1 minute or until coconut starts to brown, stirring constantly. Immediately add cereal mixture to nuts. Sprinkle cereal mixture with orange rind; add cherries, and toss well. Cool completely. Store in an airtight container. Serves 12 (serving size: ⅓ cup)

CALORIES 103; **FAT** 4.2g (sat 0.8g, mono 2.2g, poly 1.1); **PROTEIN** 3.2g; **CARB** 13.8g; **FIBER** 3g; **CHOL** 0mg; **IRON** 0.6mg; **SODIUM** 27mg; **CALC** 23mg

total time
21 min.

Fresh orange rind adds a unique sweetness to this hearty breakfast combination.

DAIRY FREE

carbs: 6g ■ fat: 7.2g
fiber: 1.8g ■ protein: 3.1g

Chili-Spiced Almonds

1 tablespoon water
1 large egg white
1 pound raw, unblanched almonds
½ cup sugar
2½ teaspoons salt
1 teaspoon Spanish smoked paprika
1 teaspoon ground cumin
1 teaspoon ground coriander
½ teaspoon chili powder
Cooking spray

1. Preheat oven to 300°.

2. Combine 1 tablespoon water and egg white in a large bowl; stir with a whisk until foamy. Add almonds; toss well to coat. Place almonds in a colander, and drain 5 minutes.

3. Combine almonds, sugar, and next 5 ingredients (through chili powder) in a large bowl; toss to coat. Spread almond mixture in a single layer on a jelly-roll pan coated with cooking spray. Bake at 300° for 15 minutes. Stir almond mixture; reduce oven temperature to 275°. Bake an additional 40 minutes, stirring every 10 minutes. Remove from oven; cool for 5 minutes. Break apart any clusters. Cool completely. Serves 32 (serving size: 2 tablespoons)

CALORIES 98; **FAT** 7.2g (sat 0.5g, mono 4.5g, poly 3.1g); **PROTEIN** 3.1g; **CARB** 6g; **FIBER** 1.8g; **CHOL** 0mg; **IRON** 0mg; **SODIUM** 181mg; **CALC** 1mg

total time
1 hr. 10 min.

Use dulce Spanish smoked paprika for a mild flavor; use picante if you want a hot flavor.

DAIRY FREE

GLUTEN FREE

carbs: 22.5g ▪ fat: 4.6g
fiber: 2.1g ▪ protein: 2.7g

Cranberry-Almond Cereal Bars

total time
1 hr. 34 min.

½ cup almond butter
⅔ cup honey
5 cups crispy wheat cereal squares
¾ cup sweetened dried cranberries

½ cup slivered almonds, toasted
Cooking spray

Be sure to stir the almond butter before measuring it to reincorporate any of the separated oil.

DAIRY FREE

PRE-WORKOUT

1. Place almond butter and honey in a large Dutch oven. Bring to a boil over medium heat. Stir in cereal, cranberries, and almonds, tossing to coat.

2. Spoon mixture into an 11 x 7-inch baking dish coated with cooking spray, pressing into an even layer with plastic wrap. Let stand 1 hour or until set. Cut into 24 bars. Serves 24 (serving size: 1 bar)

CALORIES 134; **FAT** 4.6g (sat 0.5g, mono 2.8g, poly 1.1g); **PROTEIN** 2.7g; **CARB** 22.5g; **FIBER** 2.1g; **CHOL** 0mg; **IRON** 4.1mg; **SODIUM** 134mg; **CALC** 47mg

carbs: 4.3g ▪ fat: 0.3g
fiber: 0.7g ▪ protein: 1.2g

Crispy Kale Snacks

1 (8½-ounce) bunch kale
Olive oil–flavored cooking
   spray

½ teaspoon no-salt-added
   lemon pepper seasoning
⅜ teaspoon kosher salt

1. Preheat oven to 350°.

2. Remove stems from kale; discard stems, and tear leaves into large pieces. Wash kale in a salad spinner; spin dry, and drain. Arrange kale on a large baking sheet coated with cooking spray; coat kale with cooking spray.

3. Place pan on bottom oven rack, and immediately reduce oven temperature to 300°. Bake at 300° for 20 minutes or until kale is crisp and dark green. (Do not overcook, or the leaves will turn brown.)

4. Transfer kale to a large plate lined with paper towels. Sprinkle with lemon pepper and salt. Serves 4 (serving size: ¼ of kale snacks)

CALORIES 21; **FAT** 0.3g (sat 0g, mono 0g, poly 0.1g); **PROTEIN** 1.2g; **CARB** 4.3g; **FIBER** 0.7g; **CHOL** 0mg; **IRON** 0.6mg; **SODIUM** 181mg; **CALC** 50mg

total time
25 min.

Enjoy these crunchy, seasoned kale leaves as an alternative to potato chips.

DAIRY FREE

GLUTEN FREE

LOW-CARB

PRE-WORKOUT

carbs: 12.7g ■ fat: 4g ■ fiber: 2.8g ■ protein: 3.9g

Crispy Spiced Chickpeas

1 (15-ounce) can no-salt-added chickpeas (garbanzo beans), rinsed and drained
1 tablespoon olive oil
¼ teaspoon salt
¼ teaspoon ground cumin
¼ teaspoon ground coriander
⅛ teaspoon ground cardamom
⅛ teaspoon ground red pepper

1. Preheat oven to 425°.

2. Combine all ingredients in a medium bowl, tossing well to coat. Spoon beans onto a jelly-roll pan. Bake at 425° for 45 minutes or until crisp and dry, stirring every 15 minutes. Let cool 20 minutes before serving. Serves 4 (serving size: 3 tablespoons)

CALORIES 102; **FAT** 4g (sat 0.5g, mono 2.6g, poly 0.6g); **PROTEIN** 3.9g; **CARB** 12.7g; **FIBER** 2.8g; **CHOL** 0mg; **IRON** 0.8mg; **SODIUM** 164mg; **CALC** 29mg

total time
1 hr. 10 min.

This Middle Eastern-inspired snack is a great alternative to nuts. It offers the satisfying crunch of nuts without as much fat.

DAIRY FREE

GLUTEN FREE

POST-WORKOUT

ENERGY SUSTAINING

carbs: 7.4g ▪ **fat:** 4.3g
fiber: 0.6g ▪ **protein:** 1.5g

Crostini with Sun-Dried Tomato-Olive Tapenade

1 garlic clove, halved
⅔ cup pitted kalamata olives
   (24 olives)
1 tablespoon oil from
   sun-dried tomatoes
⅓ cup drained oil-packed
   sun-dried tomato halves
   (about 8)
1 teaspoon thyme leaves

½ teaspoon grated lemon
   rind
¼ teaspoon freshly ground
   black pepper
18 (¼-inch-thick) slices
   diagonally cut French
   bread baguette, toasted

1. Drop garlic clove through food chute with food processor on, and process until minced. Add olives and next 5 ingredients (through pepper); pulse 10 times or until minced. Spread 2 teaspoons tapenade on each baguette slice. Serves 9 (serving size: 2 topped crostini)

CALORIES 73; **FAT** 4.3g (sat 0.6g, mono 3.1g, poly 0.5g); **PROTEIN** 1.5g; **CARB** 7.4g; **FIBER** 0.6g; **CHOL** 0mg; **IRON** 0.5mg; **SODIUM** 190mg; **CALC** 11mg

MAKE IT A MEAL (see page 218 for complete nutrition)

| 4 ounces grilled salmon served over 2 cups mixed salad greens | ➕ | 2 tablespoons light balsamic dressing | ➕ | 1 serving Crostini with Sun-Dried Tomato–Olive Tapenade |

total time
17 min.

For a fast entrée option, spoon the tapenade over grilled tuna or chicken, or toss with pasta.

DAIRY FREE

carbs: 6.2g ∎ fat: 3.8g
fiber: 1.2g ∎ protein: 2.2g

Curried Chutney-Stuffed Celery

6 tablespoons (4 ounces) ⅓-less-fat cream cheese, softened

2 tablespoons mango chutney

1 teaspoon grated onion

½ teaspoon red curry powder

9 celery stalks, each cut into 3 pieces

2 tablespoons finely chopped honey-roasted peanuts

1. Combine first 4 ingredients in a small bowl; stir well. Spread about 1½ teaspoons cheese mixture into each celery piece. Sprinkle cheese mixture evenly with peanuts. Serve immediately, or cover and chill. Serves 9 (serving size: 3 stuffed celery pieces)

CALORIES 66; **FAT** 3.8g (sat 1.8g, mono 1.2g, poly 0.4g); **PROTEIN** 2.2g; **CARB** 6.2g; **FIBER** 1.2g; **CHOL** 9mg; **IRON** 0.3mg; **SODIUM** 134mg; **CALC** 35mg

total time
10 min.

Walnuts are a delicious substitute if you don't have honey-roasted peanuts on hand.

MAKE IT A MEAL *(see page 218 for complete nutrition)*

| Turkey sandwich made with 2 slices whole-wheat bread; 2 ounces lean, lower-sodium deli turkey breast; lettuce leaf; and tomato slice | ➕ | 1 medium apple | ➕ | 1 serving Curried Chutney-Stuffed Celery |

carbs: 13.5g ▪ fat: 8g

fiber: 2.3g ▪ protein: 4.1g

Dill Snack Mix

2 cups crispy wheat cereal squares
1 cup mini-pretzels
½ cup slivered almonds, toasted
½ cup lightly salted dry-roasted peanuts

2 tablespoons olive oil
2 tablespoons chopped fresh dill
⅛ teaspoon kosher salt

1. Combine first 4 ingredients in large bowl.

2. Heat a small skillet over medium heat. Add oil; swirl to coat. Add dill and salt; cook 1 minute, stirring constantly. Pour dill mixture over cereal mixture; toss to coat. Serves 12 (serving size: ⅓ cup)

CALORIES 136; **FAT** 8g (sat 1g, mono 3.7g, poly 1.9g); **PROTEIN** 4.1g; **CARB** 13.5g; **FIBER** 2.3g; **CHOL** 0mg; **IRON** 3.5mg; **SODIUM** 198mg; **CALC** 37mg

total time
9 min.

Make this tasty snack mix using wheat, rice, or corn cereal squares.

DAIRY FREE

carbs: 8.5g ∎ fat: 1.2g
fiber: 0.4g ∎ protein: 3.5g

Feta Pita Crisps

3 (6-inch) pitas
1 (3.5-ounce) package
   crumbled reduced-fat
   feta cheese, finely
   chopped

Olive oil–flavored cooking
   spray

1. Preheat oven to 425°.

2. Split pitas; cut each into 4 wedges. Arrange pita wedges in a single layer on a large baking sheet; sprinkle with cheese, and lightly coat with cooking spray.

3. Bake at 425° for 10 minutes or until crisp and golden. Serves 8 (serving size: 3 pita crisps)

CALORIES 58; **FAT** 1.2g (sat 0.7g, mono 0.3g, poly 0.1g); **PROTEIN** 3.5g; **CARB** 8.5g; **FIBER** 0.4g; **CHOL** 2mg; **IRON** 0.7mg; **SODIUM** 154mg; **CALC** 34mg

total time
14 min.

**Crumble your
own block of
feta cheese for
better flavor.**

POST-WORKOUT

carbs: 7.4g ▪ fat: 2.9g ▪ protein: 0.6g
fiber: 0.9g ▪

Sweet and Spicy Kettle Corn

½ teaspoon ground red pepper
1¼ teaspoons fine sea salt
¼ teaspoon ground chipotle chile pepper

3 tablespoons canola oil
½ cup popcorn, unpopped
¼ cup sugar

1. Combine first 3 ingredients in a small bowl.

2. Heat a large Dutch oven over medium heat. Add oil; swirl to coat. Add popcorn; cover and cook 30 seconds. Sprinkle popcorn with sugar; cover. As soon as kernels begin to pop, begin shaking pan. Cook, shaking pan constantly, 4 minutes or until popping slows to 2 to 3 seconds between pops. Transfer popped corn to a large bowl. Sprinkle with red pepper mixture; toss well. Serves 16 (serving size: 1 cup)

CALORIES 57; **FAT** 2.9g (sat 0.2g, mono 1.7g, poly 0.9g); **PROTEIN** 0.6g; **CARB** 7.4g; **FIBER** 0.9g; **CHOL** 0mg; **IRON** 0.2mg; **SODIUM** 175mg; **CALC** 0mg

total time
7 min.

Popped corn keeps fresh for a day or two if stored in a paper bag with the top folded down.

DAIRY FREE

GLUTEN FREE

carbs: 11.5g ■ fat: 1g ■ fiber: 0.5g ■ protein: 2g

Veggie Tortilla Chips

2 (8½-inch) vegetable-flavored flour tortillas

Cooking spray
⅛ teaspoon salt

1. Preheat oven to 425°.

2. Lightly coat both sides of tortillas with cooking spray; cut each tortilla into 8 wedges. Place wedges on a baking sheet; sprinkle with salt. Bake at 425° for 9 minutes or until crisp, turning once. Serves 4 (serving size: 4 chips)

CALORIES 60; **FAT** 1g (sat 0.3g, mono 0.2g, poly 0.1g); **PROTEIN** 2g; **CARB** 11.5g; **FIBER** 0.5g; **CHOL** 0mg; **IRON** 1.4mg; **SODIUM** 125mg; **CALC** 50mg

total time
11 min.

By making tortilla chips yourself, you control the sodium without compromising flavor.

DAIRY FREE

PRE-WORKOUT

carbs: 15g ■ fat: 3.2g ■ fiber: 1g ■ protein: 4g

Honey-Drizzled Cherry, Goat Cheese, and Pistachio Crostini

4 ounces goat cheese, softened

½ teaspoon grated orange rind

¼ teaspoon salt

¼ teaspoon freshly ground black pepper

12 (½-inch-thick) diagonally cut French bread baguette slices, toasted

1 cup chopped pitted fresh cherries

¼ cup chopped pistachios

2 tablespoons honey

1. Combine first 4 ingredients in a small bowl. Spread goat cheese mixture evenly on one side of each toast slice. Top evenly with cherries and pistachios. Drizzle evenly with honey. Serves 12 (serving size: 1 crostino)

CALORIES 103; **FAT** 3.2g (sat 1.5g, mono 1.1g, poly 0.4g); **PROTEIN** 4g; **CARB** 15g; **FIBER** 1g; **CHOL** 4mg; **IRON** 0.9mg; **SODIUM** 189mg; **CALC** 18mg

total time
10 min.

You can easily prepare this appetizer any time of year using thawed frozen cherries.

POST-WORKOUT

carbs: 18.6g ■ **fat:** 5.5g
fiber: 2g ■ **protein:** 3.3g

Peanut-Raisin Snack Mix

1½ cups oatmeal squares cereal
1 cup toasted multigrain cereal
½ cup honey-roasted peanuts
½ cup classic granola
2 tablespoons butter, melted
½ teaspoon ground cinnamon
Cooking spray
⅓ cup raisins
⅓ cup golden raisins

total time
19 min.

Keep a container of this snack mix at the office to curb afternoon munchies.

1. Combine first 4 ingredients in large microwave-safe bowl. Combine butter and cinnamon in a small bowl. Drizzle butter mixture over cereal mixture; toss to coat. Coat mixture with cooking spray. Microwave at HIGH 3 minutes, stirring every 45 seconds. Stir in all raisins. Spread snack mix on wax paper to cool completely. Serves 12 (serving size: about 5 tablespoons)

CALORIES 131; **FAT** 5.5g (sat 1.8g, mono 2.1g, poly 1.3g); **PROTEIN** 3.3g; **CARB** 18.6g; **FIBER** 2g; **CHOL** 5mg; **IRON** 4.1mg; **SODIUM** 86mg; **CALC** 29mg

MAKE IT A MEAL (see page 218 for complete nutrition)

2 servings Peanut-Raisin Snack Mix ➕ 1 Go-Getter Green Smoothie, page 31

carbs: 12.3g ▪ **fat:** 1.1g
fiber: 0.6g ▪ **protein:** 1.2g

Ranch Snack Mix

8¼ cups (9 ounces) crispy corn cereal squares (such as Corn Chex)

2 cups fish-shaped cheddar crackers (such as Goldfish)

Cooking spray

1 tablespoon dry ranch dressing mix

1½ teaspoons dried dill

1. Preheat oven to 375°.

2. Place cereal and crackers in a large bowl. Coat mixture generously with cooking spray; toss. Sprinkle dressing mix and dill over snack mixture; toss gently, coating with cooking spray to adhere dressing mix. Spread mixture on a large baking sheet.

3. Bake at 375° for 10 minutes or until toasted, stirring after 5 minutes. Serves 24 (serving size: ¼ cup)

CALORIES 72; **FAT** 1.1g (sat 0.1g, mono 0.4g, poly 0.4g); **PROTEIN** 1.2g; **CARB** 12.3g; **FIBER** 0.6g; **CHOL** 0mg; **IRON** 3.4mg; **SODIUM** 166mg; **CALC** 45mg

total time
13 min.

Treat yourself to this filling mix when you crave a salty snack.

PRE-WORKOUT

carbs: 18.7g ▪ fat: 6.5g
fiber: 1.9g ▪ protein: 3.2g

Smoky Herbed Snack Mix

total time
1 hr. 20 min.

Fresh rosemary makes this snack mix more flavorful than prepackaged mixes.

4   cups crispy corn and rice cereal squares
½   cup small salted pretzel sticks
½   cup bite-sized reduced-fat cheddar cheese crackers
½   cup whole natural almonds, coarsely chopped

3   tablespoons light butter, melted
1   tablespoon chopped fresh rosemary
1   teaspoon smoked paprika
¼   teaspoon salt
    Cooking spray
1   cup dried apricots, coarsely chopped

1. Preheat oven to 250°.

2. Combine first 4 ingredients in a bowl. Combine butter and next 3 ingredients (through salt); drizzle over cereal mixture, tossing to coat.

3. Spread mixture into a jelly-roll pan coated with cooking spray. Bake at 250° for 45 minutes or until crisp, stirring twice. Place pan on a wire rack; gently stir in apricots. Cool completely on wire rack. Store snack mix in an airtight container up to 1 week. Serves 14 (serving size: ½ cup)

CALORIES 140; **FAT** 6.5g (sat 1.4g, mono 3.4g, poly 1.2g); **PROTEIN** 3.2g; **CARB** 18.7g; **FIBER** 1.9g; **CHOL** 3mg; **IRON** 3.9mg; **SODIUM** 198mg; **CALC** 34mg

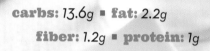

carbs: 13.6g ▪ **fat:** 2.2g
fiber: 1.2g ▪ **protein:** 1g

Spiced Sweet Potato Chips

¼ cup light sour cream
¼ cup reduced-fat mayonnaise
1 tablespoon honey
1 teaspoon grated lime rind
⅛ teaspoon salt

¼ teaspoon ground ginger
¼ teaspoon ground cinnamon
⅛ teaspoon ground red pepper
1 sweet potato
Cooking spray

1. Combine first 4 ingredients; cover and chill. Combine salt and next 3 ingredients (through red pepper); set aside.

2. Cut potato into ⅛-inch-thick slices. Place ¼ of slices in a single layer on a microwave-safe plate; coat both sides of slices with cooking spray. Sprinkle evenly with ¼ of spice mixture. Microwave at HIGH 2 to 3 minutes; turn slices, and microwave 1½ to 3 minutes or until crisp but not browned. Place on a wire rack to cool completely. Repeat procedure with remaining potato slices, cooking spray, and spice mixture.

3. Serve with sour cream mixture. Serves 6 (serving size: about 12 chips and 1½ tablespoons dip)

CALORIES 75; **FAT** 2.2g (sat 0.9g, mono 0.4g, poly 0.6g); **PROTEIN** 1g; **CARB** 13.6g; **FIBER** 1.2g; **CHOL** 3mg; **IRON** 0.4mg; **SODIUM** 156mg; **CALC** 13mg

total time
38 min.

Each microwave operates a little differently, so watch the potatoes while they cook, and adjust the cook time as needed.

GLUTEN FREE

PRE-WORKOUT

MAKE IT A MEAL *(see page 218 for complete nutrition)*

| 3 ounces grilled or baked teriyaki-flavored pork tenderloin |  | 2 servings Spiced Sweet Potato Chips | | 1 cup steamed broccoli florets |

carbs: 27.3g ■ fat: 2.6g
fiber: 3.6g ■ protein: 4.2g

Strawberry-Cereal Snack Bars

1 (10.5-ounce) package miniature marshmallows
¼ cup butter
6 cups bran twigs, soy grahams, and puffed whole-grain cereal
1 (5-ounce) package dried strawberries, chopped
Cooking spray

total time
14 min.

You can make your own variation by substituting other dried fruit for the strawberries.

1. Place marshmallows and butter in a large microwave-safe bowl. Microwave at HIGH 2 minutes. Stir until marshmallows melt. Stir in cereal and strawberries until completely coated.

2. Press mixture into a 13 x 9–inch pan coated with cooking spray. Let stand until firm. Cut into 20 bars. Serves 20 (serving size: 1 bar)

CALORIES 145; **FAT** 2.6g (sat 1.5g, mono 0.6g, poly 0.2g); **PROTEIN** 4.2g; **CARB** 27.3g; **FIBER** 3.6g; **CHOL** 6.1mg; **IRON** 1.0mg; **SODIUM** 65mg; **CALC** 26mg

---

MAKE IT A MEAL (see page 218 for complete nutrition)

| 1 serving Strawberry-Cereal Snack Bars | + | 1 cup fat-free milk | + | 1 cup blueberries |

---

carbs: 6.5g ▪ fat: 6.1g
fiber: 0.9g ▪ protein: 1.9g

Sugared Spicy Nuts

total time
21 min.

1 cup whole natural almonds
½ cup walnut halves
½ cup cashews
2 tablespoons butter
½ cup packed light brown sugar

1 tablespoon water
¼ teaspoon ground red pepper
¼ teaspoon salt
2 teaspoons chopped fresh thyme
Cooking spray

1. Place nuts in a large skillet. Cook over medium heat 8 minutes or until toasted, stirring often. Transfer to a small bowl.

2. Add butter and next 4 ingredients (through salt) to pan. Cook over medium heat 1 minute, stirring until sugar dissolves. Add nuts and thyme, stirring to coat. Cook an additional 2 minutes or until nuts are glazed and golden brown.

3. Spread mixture in a single layer on a foil-lined baking sheet coated with cooking spray. Cool completely. Serves 26 (serving size: 2 tablespoons)

CALORIES 83; **FAT** 6.1g (sat 1.1g, mono 2.8g, poly 1.8g); **PROTEIN** 1.9g; **CARB** 6.5g; **FIBER** 0.9g; **CHOL** 2mg; **IRON** 0.5mg; **SODIUM** 32mg; **CALC** 22mg

Store raw nuts in your freezer to keep them fresh longer. For this recipe, let them come to room temperature first, or toast them a minute longer.

GLUTEN FREE

Spicy Tortilla Strips

6 (8-inch) flour tortillas
Cooking spray
1½ tablespoons canola oil
⅜ teaspoon ground cumin

⅛ teaspoon ground red
pepper

1. Preheat oven to 400°.

2. Cut tortillas in half, and cut each half into 5 strips to form 60 strips. Divide tortilla strips evenly among 2 baking sheets lined with parchment paper and coated with cooking spray. Brush strips evenly with canola oil. Combine cumin and red pepper in a small bowl, and sprinkle over strips. Bake at 400° for 10 minutes or until browned, rotating baking sheets after 5 minutes. Serves 10 (serving size: 6 chips)

CALORIES 106; **FAT** 4.3g (sat 0.7g, mono 2.4g, poly 1.0g); **PROTEIN** 2.3g; **CARB** 14.2g; **FIBER** 0.9g; **CHOL** 0mg; **IRON** 1.0mg; **SODIUM** 176mg; **CALC** 36mg

total time
10 min.

Blend regular flour, whole-wheat flour, and corn tortillas for a fun mixture.

DAIRY FREE

carbs: 2.2g ▪ fat: 6.5g
fiber: 0.6g ▪ protein: 4.4g

Sweet and Spicy Pumpkinseeds

total time
17 min.

For even more kick, add an extra ⅛ teaspoon ground red pepper.

DAIRY FREE

GLUTEN FREE

LOW-CARB

1 cup unsalted pumpkinseed kernels
1 tablespoon canola oil
1 teaspoon sugar
½ teaspoon ground cumin
½ teaspoon chipotle chile powder
¼ teaspoon kosher salt
¼ teaspoon ground cinnamon
Dash of ground red pepper

1. Place pumpkinseeds in a large skillet over medium heat. Cook 4 minutes or until toasted, stirring constantly (seeds will pop slightly).

2. Combine canola oil and remaining ingredients in a large bowl; add seeds, tossing to coat. Arrange seeds in a single layer on a paper towel–lined baking sheet. Cool 10 minutes. Serves 16 (serving size: about 1 tablespoon)

CALORIES 79; **FAT** 6.5g (sat 1.2g, mono 2.3g, poly 2.8g); **PROTEIN** 4.4g; **CARB** 2.2g; **FIBER** 0.6g; **CHOL** 0mg; **IRON** 4.1mg; **SODIUM** 34mg; **CALC** 7mg

---

MAKE IT A MEAL *(see page 218 for complete nutrition)*

2 ounces skinless, chopped rotisserie chicken breast served over 2 cups mixed gourmet greens and topped with 1 ounce crumbled goat cheese	+	1 serving Sweet and Spicy Pumpkinseeds *(served over salad)*	+	2 tablespoons light raspberry vinaigrette dressing

carbs: 20g ▪ fat: 2.7g
fiber: 3.3g ▪ protein: 3.9g

Tropical Trail Mix

total time
5 min.

1 (7-ounce) package chopped dried tropical fruit

2 cups popped low-fat kettle-flavored popcorn

3 cups high-protein and high-fiber cereal

½ cup cinnamon–brown sugar–roasted almonds

1 cup fish-shaped pretzels

1. Combine all ingredients in a large bowl. Serves 16 (serving size: ½ cup)

CALORIES 111; **FAT** 2.7g (sat 0.5g, mono 1.4g, poly 0.6g); **PROTEIN** 3.9g; **CARB** 20g; **FIBER** 3.3g; **CHOL** 0mg; **IRON** 0.9mg; **SODIUM** 84mg; **CALC** 25mg

This snack couldn't be quicker or easier to make: Just stir everything together!

carbs: *4g* ▪ fat: *8.9g* ▪ fiber: *1.1g* ▪ protein: *1.6g*

Glazed Honey Nuts

1 teaspoon salt
¼ teaspoon curry powder
¼ teaspoon ground red pepper
Cooking spray

1 cup unsalted pecan halves
1 cup unsalted walnut halves
2 tablespoons honey

1. Combine salt, curry powder, and red pepper in a small bowl. Set aside.

2. Heat a large nonstick skillet over medium-high heat. Coat pan with cooking spray. Add pecans, walnuts, and honey. Cook 4 minutes or until nuts are toasted, stirring constantly. Sprinkle nuts evenly with spice mixture, tossing well to coat.

3. Spread nut mixture onto a baking sheet coated with cooking spray. Cool completely. Store in an airtight container. Serves 16 (serving size: 2 tablespoons)

CALORIES 96; **FAT** 8.9g (sat 0.8g, mono 3.3g, poly 4.4g); **PROTEIN** 1.6g; **CARB** 4g; **FIBER** 1.1g; **CHOL** 0mg; **IRON** 0.4mg; **SODIUM** 146mg; **CALC** 11mg

total time
34 min.

Spreading the nuts on a baking sheet before they're completely cooled prevents them from clumping.

DAIRY FREE

GLUTEN FREE

LOW-CARB

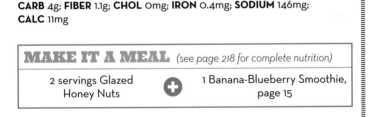

MAKE IT A MEAL *(see page 218 for complete nutrition)*

| 2 servings Glazed Honey Nuts | ➕ | 1 Banana-Blueberry Smoothie, page 15 |

carbs: 4.2g ▪ fat: 3g
fiber: 0.2g ▪ protein: 1.9g

Light **Cheese Wafers**

2 cups (8 ounces) reduced-fat shredded extra-sharp cheddar cheese
¾ cup light butter, softened
9 ounces all-purpose flour (about 2 cups)

½ teaspoon salt
½ teaspoon ground red pepper
¼ teaspoon dry mustard
¼ teaspoon smoked paprika

1. Beat cheese and butter with a mixer at medium speed until blended. Weigh or lightly spoon flour into dry measuring cups; level with a knife. Combine flour and remaining ingredients, stirring until blended. Gradually add flour mixture to butter mixture, beating until blended.

2. Shape dough into 2 (8-inch) logs; wrap in wax paper, and freeze 30 minutes or until firm enough to slice.

3. Preheat oven to 350°. Cut logs into ¼-inch slices, and place on ungreased baking sheets. Bake at 350° for 15 minutes or until lightly browned. Remove from baking sheets; cool completely on wire racks. Store in an airtight container up to 1 week. Serves 48 (serving size: 1 wafer)

CALORIES 52; **FAT** 3g (sat 1.9g, mono 0.9g, poly 0.1g); **PROTEIN** 1.9g; **CARB** 4.2g; **FIBER** 0.2g; **CHOL** 7mg; **IRON** 0.3mg; **SODIUM** 81mg; **CALC** 36mg

total time
1 hr. 20 min.

Keep a log of this dough in the freezer up to 3 months. Slice and bake as many wafers as you need when the occasion arises.

LOW-CARB

SWEET

cookies, bars, pops, and treats

slurp!

nibble!

smile!

carbs: 31.4g ▪ fat: 2.7g ▪ protein: 1.9g

fiber: 3.4g

Chewy Date-Apple Bars

2½ cups whole pitted dates
1 cup dried apples
½ cup walnuts, toasted
½ cup old-fashioned rolled oats
¼ teaspoon ground cinnamon

total time
50 min.

Try a combination of other fruit and nuts with the dates.

DAIRY FREE

1. Preheat oven to 350°.

2. Place first 3 ingredients in a food processor; process until fruit and nuts are finely chopped. Add oats and cinnamon; pulse 8 to 10 times or until moist and oats are chopped. Spoon mixture into a lightly greased 9 x 5-inch loaf pan, pressing into an even layer with plastic wrap.

3. Bake at 350° for 15 minutes. Cool completely in pan on a wire rack. Cut into 16 bars. Serves 16 (serving size: 1 bar)

CALORIES 146; **FAT** 2.7g (sat 0.3g, mono 0.5g, poly 1.9g); **PROTEIN** 1.9g; **CARB** 31.4g; **FIBER** 3.4g; **CHOL** 0mg; **IRON** 0.7mg; **SODIUM** 50mg; **CALC** 19mg

carbs: 7.4g ▪ fat: 1.4g
fiber: 0.2g ▪ protein: 0.6g

Chewy Lemon-Almond Cookies

1 (7-ounce) tube marzipan
1 cup sugar
2 large egg whites
1½ teaspoons grated lemon rind

1. Preheat oven to 300°.

2. Line 2 large baking sheets with parchment paper. Pulse marzipan and sugar in a food processor 15 times or until paste is crumbly. Add egg whites and lemon rind; process 10 seconds or until smooth.

3. Spoon batter, 1½ teaspoons at a time, 1 inch apart onto prepared baking sheets. Bake at 300° for 8 minutes, placing 1 pan on middle oven rack and other on lower oven rack. Switch pans, and bake 7 additional minutes or until puffed and golden.

4. Let cookies cool on pans 1 minute. Remove cookies from pans, and cool completely on a wire rack. Serves 40 (serving size: 1 cookie)

CALORIES 43; **FAT** 1.4g (sat 0.1g, mono 0.9g, poly 0.3g); **PROTEIN** 0.6g; **CARB** 7.4g; **FIBER** 0.2g; **CHOL** 0mg; **IRON** 0.1mg; **SODIUM** 3mg; **CALC** 9mg

total time
36 min.

Don't judge this cookie by its looks: The marzipan gives it a unique flavor that won the highest ratings in our Test Kitchens.

DAIRY FREE

GLUTEN FREE

PRE-WORKOUT

carbs: 28.8g ▪ fat: 3.1g

fiber: 0.9g ▪ protein: 2.9g

Chocolate-Granola-Yogurt Crunch Parfaits

1⅓ cups vanilla frozen fat-free yogurt

3 (0.6-ounce) dark chocolate granola thins, coarsely crushed

½ cup sliced strawberries

4 teaspoons honey

total time
6 min.

Other fruit—berries or sliced stone fruits—would be nice substitutes for the strawberries.

1. Divide frozen yogurt evenly among 4 bowls. Sprinkle granola-thin crumbs over frozen yogurt. Top with strawberries, and drizzle with honey. Serve immediately. Serves 4 (serving size: ⅓ cup frozen yogurt, 2 tablespoons crumbs, 2 tablespoons strawberries, and 1 teaspoon honey)

CALORIES 148; **FAT** 3.1g (sat 1.1g, mono 0.9g, poly 0.9g); **PROTEIN** 2.9g; **CARB** 28.8g; **FIBER** 0.9g; **CHOL** 3mg; **IRON** 0.4mg; **SODIUM** 90mg; **CALC** 78mg

MAKE IT A MEAL (see page 219 for complete nutrition)

1 slice thin-crust cheese and veggie pizza	➕	½ cup baby carrots	➕	1 serving Chocolate-Granola-Yogurt Crunch Parfait

carbs: 9.1g ▪ **fat:** 3g ▪ **fiber:** 0.9g ▪ **protein:** 1g

Chocolate-Hazelnut Popcorn

total time
49 min.

This popcorn is a healthier alternative to a candy bar.

GLUTEN FREE

Cooking spray
8 cups popcorn (popped without salt and fat)
½ cup chopped toasted hazelnuts
6 tablespoons chocolate-hazelnut spread
⅓ cup honey

1. Preheat oven to 300°.

2. Coat a large jelly-roll pan with cooking spray.

3. Place popcorn and hazelnuts on prepared pan. Combine chocolate-hazelnut spread and honey in a medium saucepan. Cook, stirring constantly, over medium-low heat 3 minutes or until melted and smooth. Drizzle hazelnut mixture over popcorn mixture, tossing gently to coat.

4. Bake at 300° for 20 minutes, stirring twice. Transfer mixture to a sheet of parchment paper; cool completely. Serves 24 (serving size: ⅓ cup)

CALORIES 67; **FAT** 3g (sat 1.5g, mono 1.1g, poly 0.3g); **PROTEIN** 1g; **CARB** 9.1g; **FIBER** 0.9g; **CHOL** 0mg; **IRON** 0.4mg; **SODIUM** 2mg; **CALC** 8mg

carbs: 15.7g • fat: 2.4g
fiber: 0.7g • protein: 1.8g

Chocolate-Raspberry Chews

1.9 ounces almond flour (about ½ cup)

1¼ cups powdered sugar, divided

3 tablespoons Dutch process cocoa

⅛ teaspoon salt

2 large egg whites

3 tablespoons low-sugar raspberry preserves

total time
62 min.

This sandwich cookie show- cases the timeless pairing of chocolate and raspberry.

DAIRY FREE

GLUTEN FREE

PRE-WORKOUT

1. Preheat oven to 325°. Weigh or lightly spoon almond flour into a dry measuring cup; level with a knife. Sift together almond flour, ¾ cup powdered sugar, and cocoa.

2. Place salt and egg whites in a medium bowl; beat with a mixer at high speed until foamy. Gradually add ½ cup pow- dered sugar, 1 tablespoon at a time, beating until stiff peaks form. Sift cocoa mixture over egg mixture; fold cocoa mixture into egg mixture. (Mixture should be smooth and shiny.)

3. Spoon dough into a pastry bag fitted with a ½-inch round tip. Pipe dough into 24 (1½-inch) rounds onto baking sheets lined with parchment paper. Sharply tap pan once on counter to remove air bubbles. Let stand 15 minutes or until surfaces of cookies begin to dry slightly.

4. Bake at 325° for 10 minutes or until cookies are crisp and firm. Cool completely on pans on wire racks. Spoon ¾ teaspoon preserves onto flat side of each of 12 cookies. Top with remaining cookies. Serves 12 (serving size: 1 sandwich cookie)

CALORIES 88; **FAT** 2.4g (sat 0.2g, mono 1.4g, poly 0.5g); **PROTEIN** 1.8g; **CARB** 15.7g; **FIBER** 0.7g; **CHOL** 0mg; **IRON** 0.6mg; **SODIUM** 36mg; **CALC** 10mg

carbs: 12.3g ▪ **fat:** 2.6g ▪ **fiber:** 0.5g ▪ **protein:** 0.8g

Chocolate-Cranberry Refrigerator Cookies

total time
1 hr. 32 min.

4.5 ounces all-purpose flour (about 1 cup)
⅓ cup unsweetened cocoa
½ teaspoon baking soda
¼ teaspoon salt
⅓ cup unsalted butter, softened

⅔ cup sugar
2 tablespoons ice water
½ cup chopped sweetened dried cranberries

Keep the dough in the refrigerator for up to one week. It's easy to slice and bake fresh cookies when the craving hits.

PRE-WORKOUT

1. Weigh or lightly spoon flour into a dry measuring cup; level with a knife. Combine flour, cocoa, baking soda, and salt in a medium bowl; stir with a whisk. Place butter and sugar in another medium bowl; beat with a mixer at medium speed until fluffy. Add flour mixture, beating at low speed until crumbly. Add 2 tablespoons ice water, 1 tablespoon at a time, beating until thoroughly moistened. Beat in cranberries.

2. Shape dough into an 8-inch log. Tightly wrap dough in plastic wrap; chill 1 hour.

3. Preheat oven to 350°.

4. Cut dough into 24 (¼-inch-thick) slices. Place slices 1 inch apart on a baking sheet lined with parchment paper. Bake at 350° for 12 minutes or until set. Cool cookies on pan 10 minutes. Remove from pan; cool completely on a wire rack. Serves 24 (serving size: 1 cookie)

CALORIES 75; **FAT** 2.6g (sat 1.5g, mono 0.6g, poly 0.1g); **PROTEIN** 0.8g; **CARB** 12.3g; **FIBER** 0.5g; **CHOL** 7mg; **IRON** 0.4mg; **SODIUM** 51mg; **CALC** 1mg

carbs: 24.2g ▪ **fat:** 2.7g
fiber: 0.2g ▪ **protein:** 3.3g

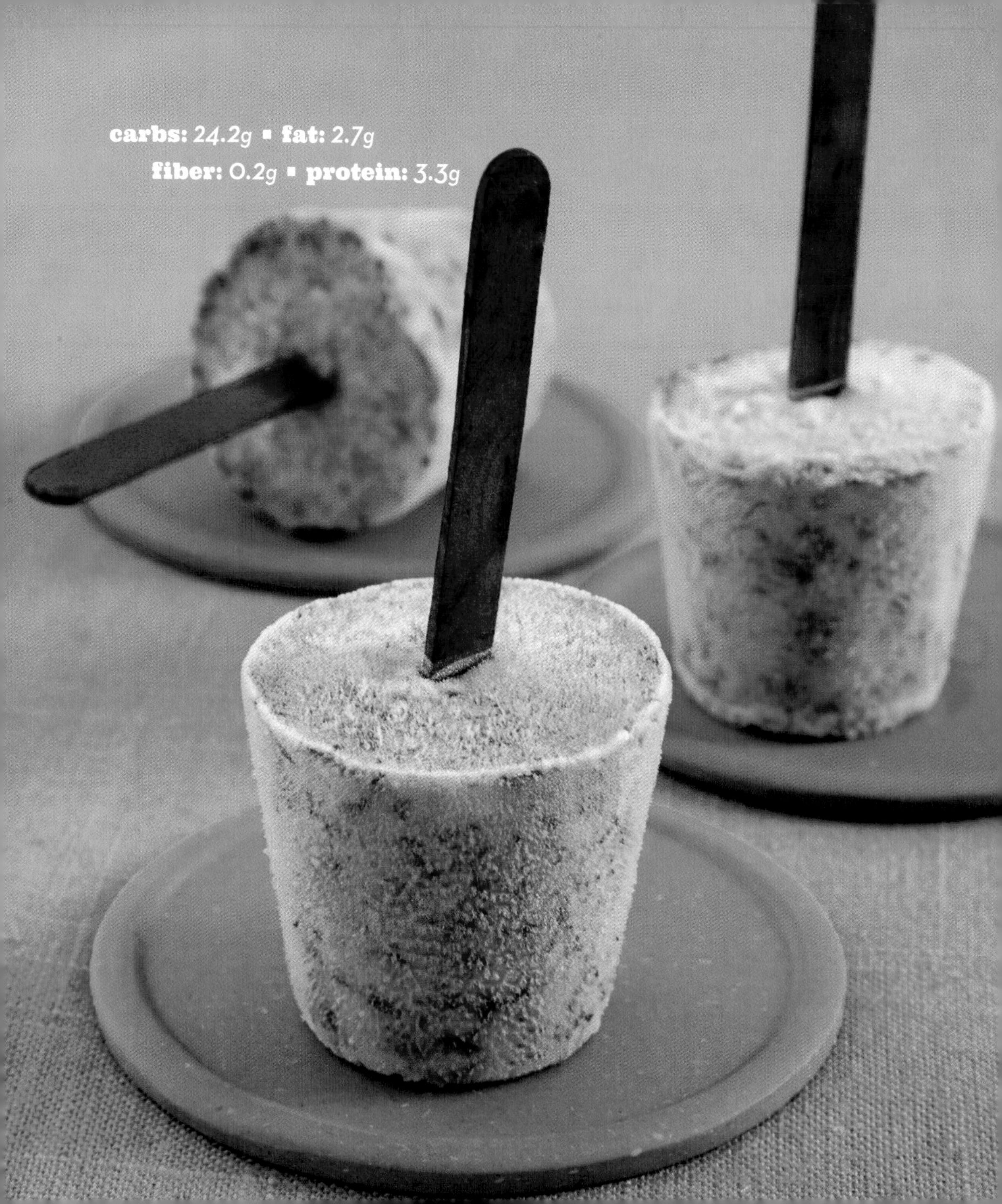

Coconut-Chocolate Freezer Pops

1 (14-ounce) can fat-free sweetened condensed milk

1 (13.5-ounce) can light coconut milk

¼ teaspoon coconut extract

1 ounce bittersweet chocolate, shaved

11 (3-ounce) paper cups

11 wooden sticks

1. Combine first 3 ingredients in a medium bowl, stirring with a whisk until smooth. Stir in chocolate.

2. Spoon mixture evenly into paper cups. Cover tops of cups with foil, and insert a wooden stick through foil into center of each cup.

3. Freeze at least 3 hours or until firm. To serve, remove foil; peel cups from pops. Serves 11 (serving size: 1 pop)

CALORIES 132; **FAT** 2.7g (sat 1.9g, mono 0.3g, poly 0.3g); **PROTEIN** 3.3g; **CARB** 24.2g; **FIBER** 0.2g; **CHOL** 5mg; **IRON** 0.2mg; **SODIUM** 89mg; **CALC** 93mg

total time
14 min. plus 3 hrs. freezing time

These decadent frozen treats will remind you of a classic chocolate-coconut candy.

GLUTEN FREE

POST-WORKOUT

carbs: 11.8g ▪ fat: 4.3g
fiber: 1.2g ▪ protein: 2.8g

Apricot-Stilton Bites

¼ cup (1 ounce) crumbled blue Stilton cheese

12 dried apricot halves

2 tablespoons coarsely chopped pistachios

1 tablespoon agave syrup

½ teaspoon chopped fresh thyme

1. Place 1 teaspoon cheese on each apricot; top each with ½ teaspoon pistachios. Drizzle evenly with syrup. Sprinkle evenly with thyme. Serves 4 (serving size: 3 topped apricots)

CALORIES 92; **FAT** 4.3g (sat 1.9g, mono 1.6g, poly 0.6g); **PROTEIN** 2.8g; **CARB** 11.8g; **FIBER** 1.2g; **CHOL** 6.3mg; **IRON** 0.4mg; **SODIUM** 144mg; **CALC** 51mg

total time
6 min.

This appetizer is also delicious with white Stilton. You can substitute honey for the agave syrup, too.

DAIRY FREE

GLUTEN FREE

Pumpkin Dip

¾ cup (6 ounces) ⅓-less-fat cream cheese

½ cup packed brown sugar

½ cup canned pumpkin

2 teaspoons maple syrup

½ teaspoon ground cinnamon

24 apple slices (3 apples)

1. Place first 3 ingredients in a medium bowl, and beat with a mixer at medium speed until well blended. Add syrup and cinnamon, and beat until smooth. Cover and chill 30 minutes. Serve with apple. Serves 12 (serving size: 2 tablespoons dip and 2 apple slices)

CALORIES 107; **FAT** 3.2g (sat 2g, mono 0.9g, poly 0.1g); **PROTEIN** 2g; **CARB** 18.3g; **FIBER** 1.4g; **CHOL** 10mg; **IRON** 1mg; **SODIUM** 87mg; **CALC** 35mg

total time
36 min.

Enjoy this super-easy pumpkin dip with fresh apple slices.

GLUTEN FREE

PRE-WORKOUT

carbs: 17.1g • fat: 2.2g
fiber: 0.2g • protein: 0.8g

Dark Chocolate-Rice Cereal Treats

1 cup bittersweet chocolate chips, divided
2 tablespoons butter
1 (10.5-ounce) package miniature marshmallows
6 cups oven-toasted rice cereal
Cooking spray

1. Place ½ cup chocolate chips, butter, and marshmallows in a medium saucepan. Cook over medium heat 3 to 4 minutes or until melted, stirring frequently.

2. Combine cereal and chocolate mixture in a large bowl, tossing to coat. Spread mixture evenly in a 13 x 9-inch metal baking pan coated with cooking spray. Let stand 15 minutes.

3. Place ½ cup chocolate chips in a microwave-safe bowl. Microwave at HIGH 1 minute, stirring after 30 seconds. Drizzle chocolate evenly over cereal mixture in pan. Let stand until cool (about 1 hour). Cut into 24 squares. Serves 24 (serving size: 1 square)

CALORIES 86; **FAT** 2.2g (sat 1.3g, mono 0.5g, poly 0.2g); **PROTEIN** 0.8g; **CARB** 17.1g; **FIBER** 0.2g; **CHOL** 3mg; **IRON** 2.4mg; **SODIUM** 69mg; **CALC** 1mg

total time
1 hr. 22 min.

All ages will go for these crisp cereal squares drizzled with a chocolate topping.

PRE-WORKOUT

carbs: *19.4g* ▪ **fat:** *6g* ▪ **fiber:** *2.1g* ▪ **protein:** *3.4g*

Frozen Peanut Butter-Banana Pops

total time
**16 min.
plus 3 hrs.
freezing time**

8 wooden sticks
4 medium-sized ripe bananas, peeled and cut in half
¼ cup fat-free milk
3 tablespoons semisweet chocolate chips
2 tablespoons creamy peanut butter
¼ cup finely chopped lightly salted peanuts

1. Line a small baking sheet with wax paper. Insert a wooden stick lengthwise into each banana half. Place bananas on prepared baking sheet; freeze 2 hours or until firm.

2. Place milk, chocolate chips, and peanut butter in a 1-cup glass measure. Microwave at HIGH 30 seconds or until hot. Stir with a whisk until smooth. Pour into a narrow glass. Let cool 5 minutes.

3. Quickly dip bananas in chocolate mixture, turning to coat; return to baking sheet. Sprinkle bananas evenly with peanuts. Freeze 1 hour or until firm. Store in freezer. Serves 8 (serving size: 1 pop)

Here's a tip for dunking the bananas: Place the chocolate mixture in a narrow glass so that when you dip the bananas, the mixture will completely coat them.

GLUTEN FREE

CALORIES 135; **FAT** 6g (sat 1.7g, mono 2.1g, poly 1.3g); **PROTEIN** 3.4g; **CARB** 19.4g; **FIBER** 2.1g; **CHOL** 0mg; **IRON** 0.3mg; **SODIUM** 60mg; **CALC** 15mg

carbs: 16.7g ■ fat: 6.9g
fiber: 1g ■ protein: 2g

Granola Cookie Wedges

Instead of scooping individual cookies, bake a superfast cookie "pie," and cut it into wedges.

⅓ cup packed dark brown sugar
2 tablespoons canola oil
1 tablespoon butter, melted
½ teaspoon vanilla extract
¼ teaspoon salt
¼ teaspoon baking soda
1 large egg white

2.25 ounces all-purpose flour (about ½ cup)
½ cup quick-cooking oats
¼ cup chopped pecans, toasted
2 tablespoons semisweet chocolate chips
Cooking spray

1. Preheat oven to 350°.

2. Combine first 7 ingredients in a large bowl; stir until well combined. Weigh or lightly spoon flour into a dry measuring cup; level with a knife. Add flour, oats, nuts, and chocolate chips to sugar mixture; stir until just combined.

3. Scrape dough into a 9-inch glass pie plate coated with cooking spray, and spread to edges using a spatula. Bake at 350° for 13 minutes or until set. Cool slightly on a wire rack. Cut into 10 wedges. Serves 10 (serving size: 1 wedge)

CALORIES 134; **FAT** 6.9g (sat 1.5g, mono 3.4g, poly 1.4g); **PROTEIN** 2g; **CARB** 16.7g; **FIBER** 1g; **CHOL** 3mg; **IRON** 0.8mg; **SODIUM** 109mg; **CALC** 14mg

MAKE IT A MEAL *(see page 219 for complete nutrition)*

1 serving Granola Cookie Wedges ➕ 1 (6-ounce) container fat-free strawberry Greek yogurt ➕ 1 cup mixed fruit and 1 small latte made with fat-free milk

carbs: 28.9g ▪ **fat:** 0g
fiber: 0.3g ▪ **protein:** 0.2g

Lemon-Basil Ice Pops

1 cup water
¾ cup sugar
3 tablespoons chopped fresh basil
1 tablespoon grated lemon rind
1 cup fresh lemon juice
6 basil leaves

1. Combine first 4 ingredients in a small saucepan. Bring to a boil; remove from heat, and let stand 30 minutes. Strain lemon mixture through a sieve into a bowl. Stir in lemon juice.

2. Pour mixture evenly into 6 (3-ounce) ice-pop molds. Place 1 basil leaf into each mold. Insert wooden stick in each mold. Freeze 8 hours or until firm. Serves 6 (serving size: 1 pop)

CALORIES 109; **FAT** 0g (sat 0g, mono 0g, poly 0g); **PROTEIN** 0.2g; **CARB** 28.9g; **FIBER** 0.3g; **CHOL** 0mg; **IRON** 0.1mg; **SODIUM** 1mg; **CALC** 8mg

total time
**38 min.
plus 8 hrs.
freezing time**

Pretty and light, these pops are a refreshing treat on a warm afternoon.

DAIRY FREE

GLUTEN FREE

PRE-WORKOUT

carbs: 8.6g ▪ fat: 2.1g ▪ fiber: 0.2g ▪ protein: 0.7g

Lemon-Cornmeal Cookies

4.5 ounces all-purpose flour
   (about 1 cup)
⅓ cup yellow cornmeal
½ teaspoon baking soda
¼ teaspoon salt
¼ teaspoon ground ginger
¾ cup plus 2 tablespoons
   sugar

6 tablespoons butter,
   softened
1 large egg
1 tablespoon grated lemon
   rind

total time
1 hr. 8 min.

Cornmeal and ginger make these cookies yield a light, subtly spiced sweet treat.

1. Preheat oven to 350°.

2. Weigh or lightly spoon flour into a dry measuring cup, and level with a knife. Combine flour and next 4 ingredients (through ginger); stir with a whisk. Combine sugar and butter in a large bowl, and beat with a mixer at medium speed until light and fluffy (about 5 minutes). Scrape sides of bowl occasionally. Add egg; beat well. Beat in grated lemon rind. Add flour mixture to butter mixture, and beat at medium-low speed just until blended.

3. Spoon about 1½ teaspoons batter 2 inches apart onto 2 parchment paper–lined baking sheets. Bake at 350° for 12 minutes or until lightly browned and almost firm. Remove from oven. Cool on pans 2 minutes or until firm. Remove from pans. Cool completely on a wire rack. Serves 36 (serving size: 1 cookie)

CALORIES 55; **FAT** 2.1g (sat 1.3g, mono 0.6g, poly 0.1g); **PROTEIN** 0.7g; **CARB** 8.6g; **FIBER** 0.2g; **CHOL** 11mg; **IRON** 0.2mg; **SODIUM** 49mg; **CALC** 2mg

carbs: 15.6g ■ fat: 0.3g

fiber: 1.3g ■ protein: 1.2g

Melon Kebabs with Lime and Chiles

5 cups cubed cantaloupe, honeydew, and watermelon
1 teaspoon grated lime rind
¼ cup fresh lime juice
1 teaspoon agave syrup
1 teaspoon crushed chipotle chile flakes
¼ teaspoon kosher salt

1. Thread 1 cup fruit onto each of 5 (8-inch) skewers, alternating cantaloupe, honeydew, and watermelon.

2. Combine lime rind, lime juice, and agave syrup in a small bowl, stirring with a small whisk. Brush syrup over fruit. Combine chile flakes and salt; sprinkle over skewers. Serves 5 (serving size: 1 kebab)

CALORIES 175; **FAT** 0.3g (sat 0.1g, mono 0g, poly 0.1g); **PROTEIN** 1.2g; **CARB** 15.6g; **FIBER** 1.3g; **CHOL** 0mg; **IRON** 0.4mg; **SODIUM** 116mg; **CALC** 15mg

total time
4 min.

These spicy kebabs, similar to those sold in the streets of Mexico, are popular with schoolchildren there—and here!

DAIRY FREE

GLUTEN FREE

PRE-WORKOUT

carbs: 2.1g ■ fat: 1.2g
fiber: 0.3g ■ protein: 2.1g

Nectarine, Prosciutto, and Arugula Bundles

Peaches or plums also work well in place of the nectarines.

DAIRY FREE

GLUTEN FREE

LOW-CARB

4 cups lightly packed trimmed arugula

1 teaspoon extra-virgin olive oil

⅛ teaspoon freshly ground black pepper

12 (½-ounce) slices prosciutto, each cut in half lengthwise

3 nectarines, each cut into 8 wedges (about ¾ pound)

1. Place first 3 ingredients in a large bowl; toss gently to combine. Arrange 3 or 4 arugula leaves at one end of 1 prosciutto strip. Place 1 nectarine wedge on top of arugula; roll up. Place bundle, seam side down, on a serving plate. Repeat procedure with remaining arugula, prosciutto, and nectarines. Serves 24 (serving size: 1 bundle)

CALORIES 26; **FAT** 1.2g (sat 0.3g, mono 0.5g, poly 0.1g); **PROTEIN** 2.1g; **CARB** 2.1g; **FIBER** 0.3g; **CHOL** 6mg; **IRON** 0.2mg; **SODIUM** 137mg; **CALC** 5mg

carbs: 26.6*g* ▪ **fat:** 2*g*
fiber: 1.2*g* ▪ **protein:** 1.6*g*

No-Bake Chocolate-Oat **Drop Cookies**

3 cups old-fashioned rolled oats

2 cups sugar

½ cup 1% chocolate low-fat milk

⅓ cup chocolate-hazelnut spread

1. Line a large baking sheet with wax paper. Place oats in a large bowl.

2. Bring sugar, chocolate milk, and hazelnut spread to a boil in a medium saucepan over high heat, stirring constantly with a whisk; boil 1½ minutes, continuing to stir constantly with a whisk. Remove from heat; pour chocolate mixture over oats, stirring to coat. Working quickly, drop oat mixture by table-spoonfuls, 1 inch apart, onto prepared baking sheet. Let cool completely. Serves 24 (serving size: 1 cookie)

CALORIES 128; **FAT** 2g (sat 1.3g, mono 0.3g, poly 0.3g); **PROTEIN** 1.6g; **CARB** 26.6g; **FIBER** 1.2g; **CHOL** 0mg; **IRON** 0.7mg; **SODIUM** 5mg; **CALC** 11mg

total time
10 min.

Look for chocolate-hazelnut spread near the peanut butter in your local grocery store.

PRE-WORKOUT

carbs: 10.7g ▪ fat: 0.6g
fiber: 0.6g ▪ protein: 2.5g

Peaches-and-Cream Ice Pops

2¼ cups chopped peeled
    ripe peaches (about
    3 large)

¼ cup sugar
1 cup vanilla 2% reduced-
    fat Greek yogurt

1. Place peaches and sugar in a medium saucepan. Bring to a simmer over medium heat, stirring frequently. Remove from heat; let cool 10 minutes.

2. Stir yogurt into peach mixture. Pour mixture evenly into 9 (3-ounce) ice-pop molds. Insert wooden sticks in each mold. Freeze according to manufacturer's directions for 8 hours or until firm. Serves 9 (serving size: 1 pop)

CALORIES 55; **FAT** 0.6g (sat 0.3g, mono 0.1g, poly 0g); **PROTEIN** 2.5g; **CARB** 10.7g; **FIBER** 0.6g; **CHOL** 2mg; **IRON** 0.1mg; **SODIUM** 8mg; **CALC** 19mg

total time
**19 min.
plus 8 hrs.
freezing time**

**Get perfect pops
by making sure
your molds are
completely dry
before you
fill them.**

GLUTEN FREE

POST-WORKOUT

MAKE IT A MEAL *(see page 219 for complete nutrition)*

3 ounces grilled chicken tenders	➕	1 medium ear of corn with 2 teaspoons butter and 1 cup green beans	➕	1 serving Peaches-and-Cream Ice Pops

carbs: 15g ▪ fat: 4.3g
fiber: 2g ▪ protein: 3.3g

Peanut Butter-
Banana Quesadilla

total time
6 min.

**This sweet
quesadilla is
wonderful as
a snack or
for dessert.**

`DAIRY FREE`

¼ cup crunchy peanut
    butter
2 (8-inch) flour tortillas
1 large ripe banana, sliced

Butter-flavored cooking spray
8 teaspoons chocolate
   syrup

1. Preheat panini grill.

2. Spread peanut butter on 1 tortilla. Arrange banana slices over peanut butter; top with remaining tortilla. Coat outsides of tortillas with cooking spray. Place quesadilla on panini grill. Cook 3 minutes or until lightly browned and crisp; cut evenly into 8 wedges. Drizzle wedges with syrup. Serves 8 (serving size: 1 wedge and 1 teaspoon syrup)

CALORIES 107; **FAT** 4.3g (sat 0.7g, mono 2.1g, poly 1.3g); **PROTEIN** 3.3g; **CARB** 15g; **FIBER** 2g; **CHOL** 0mg; **IRON** 0.4mg; **SODIUM** 110mg; **CALC** 19mg

MAKE IT A MEAL *(see page 219 for complete nutrition)*

3 servings Peanut Butter–Banana Quesadilla	➕	1 serving Tropical Trail Mix, page 101

carbs: 11.2g ■ fat: 4.6g
fiber: 0.9g ■ protein: 2.1g

Peanut Butter and Chocolate-Dipped Pretzels

4 ounces semisweet chocolate, chopped

¼ cup creamy peanut butter

30 braided honey-wheat pretzel twists

1. Line a jelly-roll pan with parchment paper.

2. Place chocolate in a small microwave-safe bowl. Microwave at HIGH 1 minute or until chocolate melts, stirring every 15 seconds. Stir in peanut butter until smooth. Working with 1 pretzel at a time, dip and roll one end of pretzel in chocolate mixture to coat. Place pretzel on prepared pan. Repeat procedure with remaining pretzels and chocolate mixture. Place in freezer for 30 minutes or until set. Serves 15 (serving size: 2 pretzels)

CALORIES 90; **FAT** 4.6g (sat 1.8g, mono 1.0g, poly 0.6g); **PROTEIN** 2.1g; **CARB** 11.2g; **FIBER** 0.9g; **CHOL** 0mg; **IRON** 0.4mg; **SODIUM** 122mg; **CALC** 2mg

total time
45 min.

Dip the pretzels, and store in the fridge on a parchment paper-lined tray up to five days ahead.

carbs: 18.4g ▪ **fat:** 7.3g
fiber: 1.7g ▪ **protein:** 2.7g

Peanut Butter-Chocolate Chip Granola Squares

Cooking spray

2 cups old-fashioned rolled oats, divided

⅓ cup sugar

¾ cup semisweet chocolate chips

⅓ cup creamy peanut butter

¼ cup honey

3 tablespoons canola oil

1. Preheat oven to 350°.

2. Coat an 8-inch square metal baking pan with cooking spray. Line pan with parchment paper, allowing paper to extend over edge of pan. Coat parchment paper with cooking spray.

3. Place ½ cup oats in a food processor; process until finely ground. Combine ground oats, 1½ cups oats, sugar, and chocolate chips in a bowl. Add peanut butter, honey, and oil; stir until a stiff dough forms. Press mixture evenly into prepared pan.

4. Bake at 350° for 25 minutes or until golden. Cool completely in pan on a wire rack. Lift mixture from pan using edges of parchment paper. Cut into 20 squares. Serves 20 (serving size: 1 square)

CALORIES 142; **FAT** 7.3g (sat 2.2g, mono 3.4g, poly 1.4g); **PROTEIN** 2.7g; **CARB** 18.4g; **FIBER** 1.7g; **CHOL** 0mg; **IRON** 0.5mg; **SODIUM** 20mg; **CALC** 2mg

total time
62 min.

By making these low-sugar granola bars at home, you can cross the sugary, store-bought variety off your grocery list.

carbs: 6.3g • fat: 3.3g
fiber: 0.4g • protein: 2g

Peanut Butter Cookies

½ cup reduced-fat creamy peanut butter

¼ cup sugar

1 large egg white

2 ounces semisweet chocolate, finely chopped

2½ tablespoons chopped lightly salted, dry-roasted peanuts

1. Combine first 3 ingredients in a large bowl; stir with a spoon just until blended. Cover and refrigerate 30 minutes.

2. Preheat oven to 325°.

3. Drop dough by half-tablespoonfuls 2 inches apart on an ungreased cookie sheet. Flatten dough gently with tines of a fork, making a crisscross pattern. Bake at 325° for 16 minutes or until lightly browned. Cool on pan 5 minutes; transfer to a wire rack.

4. While cookies cool, place chocolate in a heavy-duty zip-top plastic bag; microwave at HIGH 30 seconds or until soft. Knead bag until chocolate is smooth. Snip a tiny hole in 1 corner of bag; drizzle chocolate evenly over cookies. Sprinkle peanuts evenly over chocolate. Refrigerate 5 minutes or until chocolate is firm. Serves 24 (serving size: 1 cookie)

CALORIES 59; **FAT** 3.3g (sat 0.9g, mono 1.2g, poly 0.3g); **PROTEIN** 2g; **CARB** 6.3g; **FIBER** 0.4g; **CHOL** 0mg; **IRON** 0.2mg; **SODIUM** 48mg; **CALC** 1mg

total time
1 hr. 6 min.

There's no flour in these peanut butter cookies, which makes them gluten free and also intensifies their nutty flavor.

DAIRY FREE

GLUTEN FREE

carbs: 27.4g ▪ fat: 2.5g
fiber: 2.6g ▪ protein: 1.1g

Caramel-Apple Crunch Bars

3 tablespoons butter
½ cup caramel bits
1 (10.5-ounce) package miniature marshmallows
6 cups caramel-flavored fiber cereal, coarsely crushed
1 (5-ounce) package dried apples, chopped
Cooking spray

total time
33 min.

These bars keep well for up to three days—that is, if they last that long.

DAIRY FREE
PRE-WORKOUT

1. Melt butter in a large Dutch oven over low heat. Add caramel bits and marshmallows, stirring until marshmallows melt. Remove pan from heat. Stir in cereal and apple until thoroughly coated.

2. Press mixture into a 13 x 9-inch pan coated with cooking spray. Let stand until firm. Cut into 24 bars. Serves 24 (serving size: 1 bar)

CALORIES 133; **FAT** 2.5g (sat 1.0g, mono 0.7g, poly 0.2g); **PROTEIN** 1.1g; **CARB** 27.4g; **FIBER** 2.6g; **CHOL** 4mg; **IRON** 1.2mg; **SODIUM** 122mg; **CALC** 40mg

MAKE IT A MEAL (see page 219 for complete nutrition)

| 1 cup chicken-noodle soup | ➕ | 2 cups mixed salad greens with 2 tablespoons light Ranch dressing | ➕ | 1 serving Caramel-Apple Crunch Bars |

carbs: 15.7g • fat: 7.7g • fiber: 1.7g • protein: 3.1g

Peanutty Granola Bars

Cooking spray
2 cups old-fashioned rolled oats
1 cup unsalted, dry-roasted peanuts
1 cup flaked sweetened coconut
⅔ cup honey
¼ cup creamy peanut butter
3 tablespoons canola oil

1. Preheat oven to 325°.

2. Coat an 11 x 7–inch baking dish with cooking spray.

3. Combine oats, peanuts, and coconut on a 17½ x 12½ x 1–inch pan. Bake at 325° for 15 minutes or until lightly toasted. Transfer oat mixture to a large bowl.

4. Combine honey, peanut butter, and oil in a small saucepan. Bring to a boil over medium heat, stirring occasionally; pour over oat mixture, stirring to coat. Pour mixture into prepared dish; place heavy-duty plastic wrap on surface of mixture, and press firmly to an even thickness.

5. Bake at 325° for 10 minutes or until golden brown. Cool 1 hour or until completely cool; cut into 24 bars. (Mixture will become firm when completely cool.) Serves 24 (serving size: 1 bar)

CALORIES 137; **FAT** 7.7g (sat 1.9g, mono 3.5g, poly 2g); **PROTEIN** 3.1g; **CARB** 15.7g; **FIBER** 1.7g; **CHOL** 0mg; **IRON** 0.6mg; **SODIUM** 23mg; **CALC** 5mg

total time
1 hr. 33 min.

Using peanuts with skins adds pretty contrast to these granola bars.

`DAIRY FREE`

`GLUTEN FREE`

MAKE IT A MEAL *(see page 219 for complete nutrition)*

| 2 servings Peanutty Granola Bars | | 1 serving Blueberry-Yogurt Parfaits, page 13 |

carbs: 11.3g • fat: 4.2g
fiber: 0.7g • protein: 1.8g

Pecan Biscotti

1½ cups coarsely chopped
pecans, toasted and
divided
¾ cup sugar

9 ounces self-rising flour
(about 2 cups)
1 teaspoon vanilla extract
3 large eggs

1. Preheat oven to 350°.

2. Line a large baking sheet with parchment paper.

3. Place ½ cup pecans and sugar in a food processor; process until finely ground. Transfer pecan mixture to a large bowl. Weigh or lightly spoon flour into dry measuring cups, and level with a knife. Add flour, vanilla, and eggs to bowl. Beat with a heavy-duty mixer at medium speed just until a soft dough forms. Stir in 1 cup pecans.

4. Using floured hands, divide dough in half. Form each half into a 10 x 2-inch log. Place logs 3 inches apart on prepared baking sheet.

5. Bake at 350° for 30 minutes or until lightly browned. Cool logs on pan 10 minutes.

6. Cut logs diagonally into ¼-inch-thick slices with a serrated knife. Arrange slices on baking sheet. Bake at 350° for 10 minutes. Turn slices over; bake an additional 10 minutes or until golden and crisp. Remove slices from pan. Cool completely on a wire rack. Serves 32 (serving size: 1 biscotto)

CALORIES 88; **FAT** 4.2g (sat 0.5g, mono 2.3g, poly 1.2g); **PROTEIN** 1.8g; **CARB** 11.3g; **FIBER** 0.7g; **CHOL** 20mg; **IRON** 0.6mg; **SODIUM** 106mg; **CALC** 33mg

total time
1 hr. 35 min.

You can store these nutty biscotti for up to two weeks in an airtight container.

DAIRY FREE

carbs: 15.4g ■ fat: 2.6g ■ fiber: 0.5g ■ protein: 1.2g

Pecan-Chocolate Chip Snack Cake

2.25 ounces all-purpose flour (about ½ cup)
¼ teaspoon baking soda
¼ teaspoon salt
¾ cup packed brown sugar
1 teaspoon vanilla extract
2 large egg whites
⅓ cup chopped pecans
¼ cup semisweet chocolate chips
Cooking spray
2 teaspoons powdered sugar

1. Preheat oven to 350°.

2. Weigh or lightly spoon flour into a dry measuring cup, and level with a knife. Combine flour, baking soda, and salt in a small bowl, stirring well with a whisk. Set aside.

3. Combine brown sugar, vanilla, and egg whites in a large bowl; beat with a mixer at high speed 1 minute. Add flour mixture, beating just until combined. Stir in pecans and chocolate chips.

4. Spread batter into an 8-inch square baking pan coated with cooking spray. Bake at 350° for 18 minutes or until golden and crusty on top. Cool in pan 10 minutes. Sprinkle with powdered sugar. Cut into 16 bars. Serves 16 (serving size: 1 bar)

CALORIES 87; **FAT** 2.6g (sat 0.6g, mono 1.3g, poly 0.6g); **PROTEIN** 1.2g; **CARB** 15.4g; **FIBER** 0.5g; **CHOL** 0mg; **IRON** 0.5mg; **SODIUM** 68mg; **CALC** 12mg

total time
35 min.

You can substitute chopped walnuts, almonds, or cashews for the pecans.

PRE-WORKOUT

carbs: *12.2g* ▪ fat: *5.7g*
fiber: *0.4g* ▪ protein: *1.4g*

Pine Nut Cookies

⅓ cup almond paste
¾ cup sugar
6 tablespoons butter, softened
¼ teaspoon salt

1 large egg white
½ cup pine nuts, divided
4.5 ounces all-purpose flour (about 1 cup)
1 teaspoon baking powder

1. Preheat oven to 375°.

2. Grate almond paste on large holes of a box grater. Combine paste and next 4 ingredients (through egg white) in a large bowl; beat with a mixer at medium speed until light and fluffy (about 5 minutes).

3. Place ¼ cup pine nuts in a mini food processor; pulse until finely ground. Weigh or lightly spoon flour into a dry measuring cup; level with a knife. Combine ground nuts, flour, and baking powder, stirring with a whisk. Add flour mixture to butter mixture; beat at low speed just until combined.

4. Stack 2 baking sheets one on top of the other, and line the top sheet with parchment paper. Shape dough into 48 equal-sized balls (about 1 tablespoon each). Press 3 to 5 of the remaining pine nuts in a sunburst shape on top of each ball. Place 12 balls 2 inches apart on the top baking sheet (keep sheets stacked). Bake 14 minutes or until edges of cookies are lightly browned. Cool 5 minutes on pan. Cool completely on a wire rack. Repeat procedure 3 times. Serves 24 (serving size: 2 cookies)

CALORIES 103; **FAT** 5.7g (sat 2.0g, mono 1.8g, poly 1.3g); **PROTEIN** 1.4g; **CARB** 12.2g; **FIBER** 0.4g; **CHOL** 8mg; **IRON** 0.5mg; **SODIUM** 43mg; **CALC** 22mg

total time
1 hr. 14 min.

Almond paste is an ingenious way to flavor, tenderize, and sweeten these cookies.

carbs: 17.1g ■ fat: 1.1g fiber: 1.3g ■ protein: 4.3g

Strawberry-Ginger Yogurt Pops

2 cups quartered strawberries
¼ cup sugar
2 tablespoons water
½ teaspoon grated peeled fresh ginger
1 cup plain low-fat Greek yogurt
1 teaspoon fresh lime juice

**Spicy ginger
is the perfect
pairing with
strawberries in
these refresh-
ing yogurt pops.**

GLUTEN FREE

POST-WORKOUT

1. Combine first 4 ingredients in a medium saucepan. Bring to a boil; reduce heat, and simmer, uncovered, 5 minutes or until berries are softened, stirring occasionally. Place strawberry mixture in a blender; process until smooth. Add yogurt and lime juice. Process just until blended.

2. Fill 8 (3-ounce) ice-pop molds with strawberry mixture according to manufacturer's instructions. Freeze 8 hours or until firm. Serves 8 (serving size: 1 pop)

CALORIES 91; **FAT** 1.1g (sat 0.6g, mono 0.3g, poly 0.1g); **PROTEIN** 4.3g; **CARB** 17.1g; **FIBER** 1.3g; **CHOL** 3mg; **IRON** 0.3mg; **SODIUM** 16mg; **CALC** 41mg

carbs: 21.3g ■ fat: 3.4g fiber: 2.6g ■ protein: 1.8g

◄ Berry-Lemon Pops

1 cup measures-like-sugar sweetener	¾ cup fresh lemon juice
1 cup water	2 cups frozen whole strawberries

1. Combine first 3 ingredients in a medium saucepan. Cook over low heat, stirring until sweetener dissolves. Pour mixture into a blender. Add strawberries; process until smooth.

2. Pour mixture into 10 (3½-ounce) ice-pop molds. Top with lid; insert craft sticks. Freeze 4 hours or until thoroughly frozen. Serves 10 (serving size: 1 pop)

CALORIES 20; **FAT** 0g (sat 0g, mono 0g, poly 0g); **PROTEIN** 0.1g; **CARB** 5.2g; **FIBER** 0.4g; **CHOL** 0mg; **IRON** 0.2mg; **SODIUM** 2mg; **CALC** 7mg

total time
**12 min.
plus 4 hrs.
freezing time**

The lemonade base for these icy pops is made using a sweetener with half the calories of sugar: That's one sweet treat.

DAIRY FREE

GLUTEN FREE

PRE-WORKOUT

Trail Mix Poppers

⅔ cup sliced almonds	1 (7-ounce) bag dried fruit bits
¼ cup flaked sweetened coconut	1½ tablespoons honey

1. Place almonds in a food processor; pulse 10 times or until minced. Transfer half of almonds to a medium bowl. Add coconut and fruit bits to remaining almonds in processor; process 30 seconds or until minced. Add honey. Pulse 10 times or just until blended.

2. Using a 1-inch scoop, shape mixture into 18 (1-inch) balls. Roll balls in reserved almonds. Store in an airtight container. Serves 9 (serving size: 2 poppers)

CALORIES 119; **FAT** 3.4g (sat 0.8g, mono 1.7g, poly 0.7g); **PROTEIN** 1.8g; **CARB** 21.3g; **FIBER** 2.6g; **CHOL** 0mg; **IRON** 0.7mg; **SODIUM** 18mg; **CALC** 26mg

total time
11 min.

Pack a few of these in a snack-sized zip-top bag— they're great for a mid-hike energy boost.

DAIRY FREE

GLUTEN FREE

PRE-WORKOUT

SAVORY

Salsas, dips, chips, eggs, cheesy bites, and veggies

nips!

bites! tidbits!

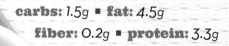

carbs: 1.5g ▪ **fat:** 4.5g
fiber: 0.2g ▪ **protein:** 3.3g

Bacon-Horseradish-Stuffed Eggs

total time
9 min.

4 hard-cooked large eggs
2 tablespoons potato flakes
2 tablespoons canola mayonnaise
1½ tablespoons minced green onions (about 1 onion)
1½ tablespoons fat-free sour cream
1 teaspoon prepared horseradish
½ teaspoon prepared mustard
¼ teaspoon freshly ground black pepper
Dash of salt
2 center-cut bacon slices, cooked and crumbled

You can prepare the eggs a day before; cover with plastic wrap, and refrigerate.

GLUTEN FREE

LOW-CARB

1. Cut eggs in half lengthwise; remove yolks. Place 2 yolks in a small bowl; reserve remaining yolks for another use. Add potato flakes and next 7 ingredients (through salt); stir until blended. Spoon 1 tablespoon egg yolk mixture into each egg white half. Sprinkle evenly with bacon. Serves 8 (serving size: 1 stuffed egg half and ¾ teaspoon bacon)

CALORIES 61; **FAT** 4.5g (sat 0.8g, mono 2.4g, poly 1.2g); **PROTEIN** 3.3g; **CARB** 1.5g; **FIBER** 0.2g; **CHOL** 50mg; **IRON** 0.3mg; **SODIUM** 116mg; **CALC** 15mg

carbs: 5.7g ■ fat: 4.1g ■ fiber: 0.1g ■ protein: 5.4g

Baked Mozzarella Bites

⅓ cup panko (Japanese breadcrumbs)
3 (1-ounce) sticks part-skim mozzarella string cheese
3 tablespoons egg substitute

Cooking spray
6 tablespoons lower-sodium marinara sauce

total time
33 min.

Serve this quick after-school snack to your kids as an alternative to traditional fried cheesesticks.

1. Preheat oven to 425°.

2. Heat a medium skillet over medium heat. Add panko to pan, and cook 2 minutes or until toasted, stirring frequently. Remove from heat, and place panko in a shallow dish.

3. Cut each mozzarella stick into 4 pieces. Working with one piece at a time, dip cheese in egg substitute; dredge in panko. Place cheese on a baking sheet coated with cooking spray. Bake at 425° for 3 minutes or until the cheese is softened and thoroughly heated.

4. Pour marinara sauce into a microwave-safe bowl. Microwave at HIGH 1 minute or until thoroughly heated, stirring after 30 seconds. Serve with mozzarella pieces. Serves 6 (serving size: 2 mozzarella bites and 1 tablespoon sauce)

CALORIES 76; **FAT** 4.1g (sat 1.8g, mono 1.3g, poly 0.3g); **PROTEIN** 5.4g; **CARB** 5.7g; **FIBER** 0.1g; **CHOL** 8mg; **IRON** 0.4mg; **SODIUM** 161mg; **CALC** 106mg

carbs: 9.2g ■ fat: 2.2g
fiber: 0.5g ■ protein: 5.2g

Barbecue Pizza Bites

½ pound ground round
½ cup chopped onion
½ cup chopped carrot
⅓ cup barbecue sauce
3 tablespoons brown sugar
¼ teaspoon salt
Dash of black pepper
4 (4-ounce) Italian pizza crusts

¼ cup (1 ounce) finely shredded provolone or part-skim mozzarella cheese
2 tablespoons chopped fresh cilantro

total time
33 min.

Use your favorite barbecue sauce to add tang, heat, and sweetness to these pizza bites.

POST-WORKOUT

1. Preheat oven to 450°.

2. Cook beef, onion, and carrot in a large nonstick skillet over medium-high heat until meat is browned, stirring to crumble. Drain well; return meat mixture to pan. Stir in barbecue sauce, sugar, salt, and pepper; reduce heat, and simmer 5 minutes.

3. Place pizza crusts on a baking sheet. Divide beef mixture evenly among crusts, and sprinkle with cheese. Bake pizzas at 450° for 12 minutes or until cheese melts. Sprinkle pizzas with cilantro. Cut each pizza into 4 wedges. Serves 16 (serving size: 1 wedge)

CALORIES 78; **FAT** 2.2g (sat 0.9g, mono 0.8g, poly 0.3g); **PROTEIN** 5.2g; **CARB** 9.2g; **FIBER** 0.5g; **CHOL** 10mg; **IRON** 0.8mg; **SODIUM** 178mg; **CALC** 57mg

---

MAKE IT A MEAL *(see page 219 for complete nutrition)*

3 servings Barbecue Pizza Bites		1 serving Peanut Butter–Banana Dip served with apples in recipe, page 41

carbs: 4.8g ▪ fat: 2.8g ▪ fiber: 0g ▪ protein: 0.9g

Brazilian Cheese Puffs

total time
38 min.

These treats are sold at snack bars in Brazil. Look for tapioca flour in large supermarkets or health food markets.

GLUTEN FREE

LOW-CARB

½ cup 1% low-fat milk
¼ cup olive oil
½ teaspoon kosher salt
1 large egg
1 garlic clove, peeled

4.2 ounces tapioca flour (about 1 cup)
¾ cup (3 ounces) crumbled queso fresco
Cooking spray

1. Preheat oven to 400°.

2. Place first 5 ingredients in a blender. Weigh or lightly spoon flour into a dry measuring cup; level with a knife. Add flour to blender; process until smooth. Add cheese; process 2 seconds. Immediately pour batter into 24 miniature muffin cups coated with cooking spray, filling two-thirds full.

3. Bake at 400° for 15 to 18 minutes or until puffed and golden. Cool 3 minutes in pans on a wire rack; remove from pans. Serve warm. Serves 24 (serving size: 1 puff)

CALORIES 47; **FAT** 2.8g (sat 0.6g, mono 1.8g, poly 0.3g); **PROTEIN** 0.9g; **CARB** 4.8g; **FIBER** 0g; **CHOL** 10mg; **IRON** 0.1mg; **SODIUM** 50mg; **CALC** 18mg

carbs: 8.9g ▪ fat: 1.7g ▪ fiber: 0.4g ▪ protein: 11.1g

Chicken Nuggets with Mustard Sauce

total time
50 min.

These healthier chicken nuggets begin with a soak in buttermilk to make the lean chicken juicy.

Chicken:
½ cup low-fat buttermilk
1½ pounds skinless, boneless chicken breast, cut into 42 pieces
3¾ cups cornflakes
1 teaspoon paprika
½ teaspoon sugar
¼ teaspoon salt
Cooking spray

Sauce:
½ cup prepared mustard
¼ cup honey
½ teaspoon grated peeled fresh ginger

1. Preheat oven to 375°.

2. To prepare chicken, combine buttermilk and chicken. Marinate in refrigerator 30 minutes; drain.

3. Place cornflakes, paprika, sugar, and salt in a food processor; process until cornflakes are finely chopped. Combine the chicken and cornflake mixture, tossing well to coat. Place chicken on a baking sheet coated with cooking spray. Bake at 375° for 15 minutes or until done.

4. Combine mustard, honey, and ginger. Serve with chicken. Serves 14 (serving size: 3 nuggets and about 1 teaspoon sauce)

CALORIES 95; **FAT** 1.7g (sat 0.3g, mono 0.5g, poly 0.3g); **PROTEIN** 11.1g; **CARB** 8.9g; **FIBER** 0.4g; **CHOL** 31mg; **IRON** 2.2mg; **SODIUM** 178mg; **CALC** 8mg

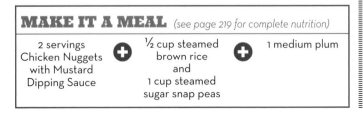

MAKE IT A MEAL *(see page 219 for complete nutrition)*

2 servings Chicken Nuggets with Mustard Dipping Sauce ➕ ½ cup steamed brown rice and 1 cup steamed sugar snap peas ➕ 1 medium plum

carbs: 2.1g ■ fat: 3.6g ■ fiber: 0.3g ■ protein: 5.3g

Egg Salad Deviled Eggs

12 hard-cooked large eggs
¼ cup drained no-salt-added chickpeas (garbanzo beans)
3 tablespoons light mayonnaise
½ teaspoon dry mustard
¼ teaspoon salt
⅛ teaspoon ground red pepper
3 tablespoons finely chopped celery
1½ tablespoons finely chopped red onion
1 tablespoon finely chopped fresh parsley

1. Cut eggs in half lengthwise; discard 6 yolks or reserve them for another use. Place remaining yolks in a medium bowl. Add chickpeas and next 4 ingredients (through red pepper); mash with a fork until smooth. Stir in celery, onion, and parsley.

2. Spoon egg mixture into a heavy-duty zip-top plastic bag. Seal bag, removing as much air as possible. Snip a small hole in 1 corner of bag. Pipe egg mixture evenly into egg whites. Serves 12 (serving size: 2 stuffed egg halves)

CALORIES 64; **FAT** 3.6g (sat 1.0g, mono 1.0g, poly 0.4g); **PROTEIN** 5.3g; **CARB** 2.1g; **FIBER** 0.3g; **CHOL** 104mg; **IRON** 0.4mg; **SODIUM** 141mg; **CALC** 17mg

total time
19 min.

These tasty deviled eggs use only a portion of the egg yolks to keep calories and fat in check.

GLUTEN FREE
LOW-CARB

carbs: 4.8g ■ fat: 2.4g ■ protein: 4g
fiber: 1.1g

Endive Spears with Spicy Goat Cheese

½ cup (4 ounces) goat cheese
⅓ cup plain fat-free Greek yogurt
¼ teaspoon kosher salt
⅛ teaspoon ground red pepper

1 garlic clove, pressed
1¼ teaspoons Hungarian sweet paprika, divided
36 Belgian endive leaves (about 3 heads)

1. Combine first 5 ingredients and 1 teaspoon paprika in a medium bowl; mash with a fork until smooth. Top each endive leaf with about 1 teaspoon cheese mixture. Sprinkle ¼ teaspoon paprika evenly over cheese mixture. Serves 12 (serving size: 3 filled leaves)

CALORIES 53; **FAT** 2.4g (sat 1.6g, mono 0.5g, poly 0.2g); **PROTEIN** 4g; **CARB** 4.8g; **FIBER** 1.1g; **CHOL** 4.7mg; **IRON** 1.3mg; **SODIUM** 105mg; **CALC** 88mg

total time
8 min.

The cheese mixture also makes a delicious sandwich or bagel spread, or a thick dip for crudités.

carbs: 7g ▪ fat: 4.1g ▪ fiber: 0.4g ▪ protein: 1.5g

Fig-Goat Cheese Phyllo Bites

total time
36 min.

Tangy goat cheese with sweet figs and crunchy, toasty walnuts create a delightful bite.

PRE-WORKOUT

1 (1.9-ounce) package mini phyllo shells
2 ounces crumbled goat cheese (about ½ cup)
2 ounces ⅓-less-fat cream cheese (about ¼ cup), softened
¼ cup fig preserves, finely chopped
¼ cup chopped dried Calimyrna figs
¼ cup chopped walnuts, toasted

1. Preheat oven to 350°.

2. Place phyllo shells on a baking sheet; bake at 350° for 3 minutes. Cool completely.

3. While shells cool, combine cheeses in a small bowl; stir well. Combine fig preserves and dried figs in a small bowl; stir well.

4. Spoon about 2 teaspoons cheese mixture into each phyllo cup; top each with 1½ teaspoons fig mixture. Sprinkle each cup with ¾ teaspoon walnuts. Serves 15 (serving size: 1 phyllo bite)

CALORIES 70; **FAT** 4.1g (sat 1.4g, mono 0.9g, poly 1.1g); **PROTEIN** 1.5g; **CARB** 7g; **FIBER** 0.4g; **CHOL** 6mg; **IRON** 0.3mg; **SODIUM** 46mg; **CALC** 20mg

---

MAKE IT A MEAL *(see page 219 for complete nutrition)*

| 2 servings Fig-Goat Cheese Phyllo Bites |  | 2 servings Pumpkin-Parmesan Hummus served with pita chips in recipe, page 43 |

---

carbs: *11.8*g ▪ **fat:** *1.2*g ▪ **fiber:** *1.6*g ▪ **protein:** *1.4*g

Fresh Salsa

1⅔ cups chopped seeded
   tomato (1 large)
½ cup chopped red onion
¼ cup chopped fresh
   cilantro
2 tablespoons fresh lime
   juice
¼ teaspoon salt

2 garlic cloves, minced
1 jalapeño pepper, seeded
   and minced
2 tablespoons sliced green
   onion tops (optional)
42 baked tortilla chips or
   tortilla chip scoops

1. Combine first 7 ingredients in a medium bowl. Stir in
the green onions, if desired. Serve with tortilla chips. Serves
7 (serving size: ¼ cup salsa and 6 chips)

CALORIES 60; **FAT** 1.2g (sat 0.2g, mono 0.3g, poly 0.1g); **PROTEIN** 1.4g;
CARB 11.8g; **FIBER** 1.6g; **CHOL** 0mg; **IRON** 0.3mg; **SODIUM** 144mg;
CALC 17mg

total time
13 min.

**Tomato seeds
can be bitter,
so remove
them: Cut the
tomato in half
horizontally,
and use a spoon
to scrape out
the seeds.**

DAIRY FREE
GLUTEN FREE
PRE-WORKOUT

carbs: 2g ■ fat: 3.9g
fiber: 0.9g ■ protein: 1.8g

Goat Cheese-Stuffed Piquillo Peppers

total time
10 min.

If you make these ahead, wait until just before serving to add the vinaigrette and chives.

GLUTEN FREE

4 teaspoons olive oil, divided
2 tablespoons chopped pitted kalamata olives
¼ teaspoon garlic pepper
1 (4-ounce) package goat cheese

1½ teaspoons sherry vinegar
1 (9.5-ounce) jar pimientos del piquillo peppers (about 12 peppers)
2 teaspoons chopped fresh chives

1. Combine 1 teaspoon oil and next 3 ingredients (through goat cheese) in a small bowl.

2. Combine 3 teaspoons oil and vinegar in another small bowl, stirring with a whisk.

3. Drain peppers and pat dry. Carefully make a vertical slit down 1 side of each pepper. Open peppers, and fill evenly with cheese mixture. Close edges of pepper over filling to seal. Place stuffed peppers, seam sides down, on a serving platter. Drizzle evenly with vinaigrette, and sprinkle evenly with chives. Serve immediately. Serves 12 (serving size: 1 pepper)

CALORIES 52; **FAT** 3.9g (sat 1.6g, mono 1.9g, poly 0.3g); **PROTEIN** 1.8g; **CARB** 2g; **FIBER** 0.9g; **CHOL** 4.4mg; **IRON** 0.2mg; **SODIUM** 128mg; **CALC** 14mg

carbs: 16.5g ▪ fat: 4.1g ▪ fiber: 2.8g ▪ protein: 2.2g

Grilled Corn, Tomatillo, and Avocado Salsa

3 tomatillos

3 ears shucked corn

Cooking spray

1 large diced peeled avocado

1 cup grape tomatoes, quartered

¼ cup chopped red onion

2 tablespoons chopped fresh cilantro

2 tablespoons fresh lime juice

½ teaspoon salt

¼ teaspoon freshly ground black pepper

60 baked tortilla chips or tortilla chip scoops

total time

25 min.

Serve this colorful salsa with baked tortilla chips, or with grilled chicken or flank steak.

DAIRY FREE

GLUTEN FREE

1. Preheat grill to high heat.

2. Discard husks and stems from tomatillos. Place tomatillos and corn on grill rack coated with cooking spray; grill 8 to 10 minutes or until tender, turning frequently.

3. While vegetables grill, combine avocado and next 6 ingredients (through pepper) in a medium bowl. Cut kernels from ears of corn and chop tomatillos; add to avocado mixture, and combine. Serve immediately, or cover and chill until ready to serve. Serve with tortilla chips. Serves 10 (serving size: ¼ cup and 6 chips)

CALORIES 103; **FAT** 4.1g (sat 0.6g, mono 1.6g, poly 0.5g); **PROTEIN** 2.2g; **CARB** 16.5g; **FIBER** 2.8g; **CHOL** 0mg; **IRON** 0.5mg; **SODIUM** 181mg; **CALC** 14mg

carbs: 5.1g ■ fat: 2.6g ■ fiber: 0.2g ■ protein: 3.7g

Ham-and-Swiss Quiche Cups

Cooking spray
12 wonton wrappers
2 large eggs
1 tablespoon light sour cream

2 ounces shredded Swiss cheese (about ½ cup)
⅓ cup finely chopped ham
Chopped green onions (optional)

1. Preheat oven to 350°.

2. Coat 2 (12-cup) muffin pans with cooking spray. Working with 1 wonton wrapper at a time (cover the remaining wonton wrappers with a damp towel to keep them from drying), press the wrappers into bottoms of every other muffin cup.

3. Combine eggs and sour cream, stirring with a whisk. Stir in cheese and ham. Spoon about 1 tablespoon egg mixture into each wonton cup. Bake at 350° for 16 to 18 minutes or until golden brown. Cool in pans 2 minutes; serve warm. Sprinkle with chopped green onions, if deisred. Serves 12 (serving size: 1 quiche cup)

CALORIES 59; **FAT** 2.6g (sat 1.3g, mono 0.7g, poly 0.2g); **PROTEIN** 3.7g; **CARB** 5.1g; **FIBER** 0.2g; **CHOL** 43mg; **IRON** 0.5mg; **SODIUM** 93mg; **CALC** 48mg

total time
38 min.

Use two muffin tins, and place a wonton in every other cup. The extra space keeps them from sticking together.

carbs: 19.6g ■ fat: 5.4g
fiber: 3.4g ■ protein: 4.2g

Hot Bean-and-Cheese Dip

1 (14.5-ounce) can diced tomatoes, drained and divided
½ teaspoon hot pepper sauce
⅛ teaspoon salt
¼ teaspoon ground cumin
¼ teaspoon dried oregano
1 (16-ounce) can pinto beans, rinsed and drained
1 (16-ounce) can fat-free refried beans
1 (4.5-ounce) can chopped green chiles, drained
Cooking spray
¾ cup (3 ounces) shredded sharp cheddar cheese
2 tablespoons chopped green onion tops (optional)
108 baked corn tortilla chips

1. Preheat oven to 350°.

2. Combine 1 cup tomatoes and next 7 ingredients (through chiles). Spoon tomato mixture into a 1½-quart casserole dish coated with cooking spray. Top with cheese. Bake at 350° for 20 minutes or until cheese is melted. Top with remaining tomatoes. Garnish with green onions, if desired. Serve with corn tortilla chips. Serves 36 (serving size: 2 tablespoons dip and 3 chips)

CALORIES 146; **FAT** 5.4g (sat 1.1 g, mono 0.5g, poly 0.1g); **PROTEIN** 4.2g; **CARB** 19.6g; **FIBER** 3.4g; **CHOL** 4mg; **IRON** 1.0mg; **SODIUM** 204mg; **CALC** 69mg

total time
28 min.

This is a perfect snack to serve for a football-watching party, too.

GLUTEN FREE

MAKE IT A MEAL *(see page 219 for complete nutrition)*

2 servings Hot Bean-and-Cheese Dip	➕	1 serving Pimiento Cheese Poppers, page 205

carbs: 3.5g • fat: 2.5g • fiber: 0.2g • protein: 1.9g

Mini Caprese Pita Crackers

12	pita crackers
¼	cup sun-dried tomato pesto
12	medium basil leaves
3	ounces fresh mozzarella cheese
2	tablespoons balsamic glaze

1. Spread pita crackers evenly with pesto; top each with 1 basil leaf.

2. Cut mozzarella into 6 thin slices; cut each slice in half. Place 1 cheese slice on top of each basil leaf; drizzle evenly with balsamic glaze. Serves 12 (serving size: 1 mini pita)

CALORIES 44; **FAT** 2.5g (sat 1.1g, mono 0.2g, poly 0.1g); **PROTEIN** 1.9g; **CARB** 3.5g; **FIBER** 0.2g; **CHOL** 6mg; **IRON** 0.3mg; **SODIUM** 81mg; **CALC** 3mg

total time
10 min.

This appetizer-sized twist on a traditional Caprese salad uses sun-dried tomato pesto instead of fresh tomatoes.

LOW-CARB

carbs: 6.4g ▪ fat: 1.9g
fiber: 0.3g ▪ protein: 1.9g

Mini Pesto Pretzels

total time
42 min.

1 (11-ounce) can refrigerated breadstick dough
⅓ cup grated fresh Parmesan cheese
3 tablespoons commercial pesto
Cooking spray

Turn breadstick dough into easy pretzels you can carry in a zip-top bag for a quick snack.

1. Preheat oven to 425°.

2. Unroll dough; separate into 12 breadsticks. Cut each breadstick in half lengthwise. Roll each breadstick half into a 16-inch rope. Cross one end of rope over the other to form a circle. Twist rope once at base of the circle. Fold ends over circle and into traditional pretzel shape, pinching gently to seal.

3. Place cheese in a shallow dish. Brush top side of pretzels evenly with pesto. Press pesto side of pretzels into cheese. Place pretzels, cheese side up, on a baking sheet coated with cooking spray.

4. Bake at 425° for 12 minutes or until golden brown.
Serves 24 (serving size: 1 pretzel)

CALORIES 51; **FAT** 1.9g (sat 0.8g, mono 0.8g, poly 0.2g); **PROTEIN** 1.9g; **CARB** 6.4g; **FIBER** 0.3g; **CHOL** 2mg; **IRON** 0.4mg; **SODIUM** 137mg; **CALC** 27mg

carbs: 13.9g ▪ **fat:** 2.4g ▪ **fiber:** 1.4g ▪ **protein:** 2.2g

Mini Cheddar Potato Skins

1 pound red fingerling
  potatoes (about 12)
1 tablespoon butter, melted
¼ teaspoon salt
¼ teaspoon freshly ground
  black pepper

Cooking spray
3 tablespoons reduced-fat
  shredded extra-sharp
  cheddar cheese
2 tablespoons thinly sliced
  green onions

1. Preheat broiler.

2. Scrub potatoes; place in a single layer in a microwave-safe bowl (do not pierce potatoes with a fork). Cover bowl with plastic wrap (do not allow plastic wrap to touch food); vent. Microwave at HIGH 5 to 6 minutes or until tender. Let stand 5 minutes or until cool enough to touch.

3. Cut potatoes in half; drizzle evenly with butter, and sprinkle evenly with salt and pepper. Lay cut sides up on a foil-lined baking sheet coated with cooking spray. Top evenly with cheese. Broil 2 minutes or until cheese melts; sprinkle evenly with green onions. Serves 8 (serving size: about 3 potato halves)

CALORIES 84; **FAT** 2.4g (sat 1.4g, mono 0.4g, poly 0.1g); **PROTEIN** 2.2g; **CARB** 13.9g; **FIBER** 1.4g; **CHOL** 7mg; **IRON** 0.5mg; **SODIUM** 124mg; **CALC** 51mg

total time
17 min.

Reduced-fat cheese and a tiny amount of butter mean that you can enjoy all the flavor of potato skins without the extra calories.

`GLUTEN FREE`

`PRE-WORKOUT`

MAKE IT A MEAL *(see page 219 for complete nutrition)*

3 ounces broiled or grilled flank steak		2 servings Mini Cheddar Potato Skins		12 steamed asparagus spears

carbs: 1.3g ∎ fat: 4.5g
fiber: 0.1g ∎ protein: 5.5g

Mozzarella-Pepper Roll-Ups

total time
8 min.

1 (12-ounce) package sheet-style mozzarella cheese
¼ teaspoon freshly ground black pepper
⅓ cup drained canned artichoke hearts, finely chopped
½ cup drained bottled roasted red bell peppers, chopped
½ cup basil leaves

Mozzarella sheets are flat sheets of cheese that make great wrappings for flavorful ingredients.

GLUTEN FREE

LOW-CARB

1. Unroll mozzarella sheet; cut in half lengthwise. Sprinkle each strip of mozzarella evenly with black pepper, artichoke hearts, and bell pepper. Lay basil leaves evenly along the top of vegetables on each strip. Roll up each strip beginning at short side; cut into 8 (1-inch) rounds. Serve immediately. Serves 16 (serving size: 1 roll-up)

CALORIES 71; **FAT** 4.5g (sat 2.6g, mono 1.2g, poly 0.2g); **PROTEIN** 5.5g; **CARB** 1.3g; **FIBER** 0.1g; **CHOL** 11mg; **IRON** 0.1mg; **SODIUM** 170mg; **CALC** 153mg

carbs: 10.5g ▪ fat: 3.4g
fiber: 1.5g ▪ protein: 4.3g

Mushroom Pizza Sticks

1 (8.8-ounce) package whole-wheat naan flatbreads, each cut into 1¼-inch strips (total of 12 strips)
Cooking spray
½ cup lower-sodium marinara sauce
½ (8-ounce) package cremini mushrooms, chopped
4 ounces shredded part-skim mozzarella cheese (about 1 cup)
Oregano leaves (optional)
Additional pizza sauce (optional)

These healthier pizza sticks are perfect for an after-school snack or a casual family gathering.

POST-WORKOUT

ENERGY SUSTAINING

1. Preheat oven to 450°.

2. Place naan strips on a baking sheet coated with cooking spray. Spread sauce evenly over strips; sprinkle with mushrooms, and top with cheese.

3. Bake at 450° for 10 minutes or until golden brown and bubbly. Garnish with oregano, and serve with additional pizza sauce, if desired. Serves 12 (serving size: 1 pizza stick)

CALORIES 91; **FAT** 3.4g (sat 1.5g, mono 0.6g, poly 0.7g); **PROTEIN** 4.3g; **CARB** 10.5g; **FIBER** 1.5g; **CHOL** 8mg; **IRON** 0.8mg; **SODIUM** 200mg; **CALC** 90mg

carbs: 14.8g ▪ **fat:** 2g ▪ **fiber:** 2.4g ▪ **protein:** 5.7g

Pear and Swiss Triangles

total time
20 min.

8 (1-ounce) slices white-wheat bread
¼ cup pear preserves
4 (¾-ounce) slices light Jarlsburg cheese
1 Anjou pear, thinly sliced
Cooking spray

Enjoy a mini grilled cheese sandwich that showcases the classic combo of pear and cheese.

POST-WORKOUT

ENERGY SUSTAINING

1. Trim crusts from bread. Spread 1 tablespoon preserves over each of 4 bread slices. Top each with 1 cheese slice. Place pear slices evenly over cheese. Top with remaining bread slices. Coat both sides of sandwiches evenly with cooking spray.

2. Heat a large nonstick skillet over medium heat. Add 2 sandwiches to pan. Cover with a sheet of foil; top with a heavy skillet. Cook 3 minutes or until lightly browned. Turn sandwiches over; replace foil and skillet. Cook 3 minutes or until golden. Repeat procedure with remaining sandwiches. Cut each sandwich diagonally into 4 triangles. Serve immediately. Serves 8 (serving size: 2 triangles)

CALORIES 91; **FAT** 2g (sat 0.9g, mono 0.3g, poly 0.3g); **PROTEIN** 5.7g; **CARB** 14.8g; **FIBER** 2.4g; **CHOL** 5mg; **IRON** 1.3mg; **SODIUM** 136mg; **CALC** 206mg

MAKE IT A MEAL (see page 219 for complete nutrition)

| 3 servings Pear and Swiss Triangles | ➕ | 1 serving Lemony Fruit Dip served with strawberries in recipe, page 39 |

carbs: 2.1g ■ fat: 5.3g ■ protein: 3.5g
fiber: 0.4g

Pimiento Cheese Poppers

3 ounces ⅓-less-fat cream cheese, softened
3 ounces fat-free cream cheese, softened
8 ounces reduced-fat extra-sharp cheddar cheese, shredded
¼ cup canola mayonnaise

1 (4-ounce) jar diced pimientos, drained
2 tablespoons finely diced onion
Ground red pepper (optional)
24 tricolor sweet mini peppers, cut in half

1. Combine first 6 ingredients and ground red pepper, if desired, in a medium bowl. Stuff each pepper half with 2 teaspoons cheese mixture. Refrigerate until ready to serve. Serves 24 (serving size: 2 stuffed pepper halves)

CALORIES 72; **FAT** 5.3g (sat 2.0g, mono 2.4g, poly 0.9g); **PROTEIN** 3.5g; **CARB** 2.1g; **FIBER** 0.4g; **CHOL** 11mg; **IRON** 0.1mg; **SODIUM** 142mg; **CALC** 84mg

total time
9 min.

Pimiento cheese is a great snack with any fresh veggie. Try it with celery sticks or bell pepper wedges.

GLUTEN FREE
LOW-CARB

carbs: 28g ▪ fat: 2.6g
fiber: 0.5g ▪ protein: 1.1g

◀ Plantain Chips

1	tablespoon olive oil	¼	teaspoon salt
2	medium plantains, peeled and cut into ¼-inch diagonal slices (about 2 cups)	⅛	teaspoon ground red pepper

1. Heat a large nonstick skillet over medium heat. Add oil; swirl to coat. Add plantain slices; cook 3 minutes on each side or until browned. Sprinkle salt and pepper over chips. Serves 6 (serving size: ⅓ cup)

CALORIES 127; **FAT** 2.6g (sat 0.3g, mono 1.7g, poly 0.2g); **PROTEIN** 1.1g; **CARB** 28g; **FIBER** 0.5g; **CHOL** 0mg; **IRON** 0.5mg; **SODIUM** 101mg; **CALC** 3mg

total time
11 min.

Serve plantain chips alone or with a dip like guacamole.

DAIRY FREE

GLUTEN FREE

PRE-WORKOUT

Tofu Bites

1	pound extra-firm reduced-fat water-packed tofu, drained and cut into ½-inch cubes	1	teaspoon dark sesame oil
1½	teaspoons canola oil	2	tablespoons low-sodium soy sauce
		1	tablespoon rice vinegar

1. Place tofu on several layers of heavy-duty paper towels. Cover tofu with additional paper towels, and let stand 5 minutes, pressing occasionally.

2. Heat a large nonstick skillet over medium-high heat. Add oils to pan; swirl to coat. Add tofu; sauté 7 minutes or until browned. Place in a bowl. Drizzle with soy sauce and vinegar; toss gently to coat. Cover and chill at least 1 hour, stirring occasionally. Serves 8 (serving size: ¼ cup)

CALORIES 38; **FAT** 2.1g (sat 0.2g, mono 0.8g, poly 0.9g); **PROTEIN** 3.6g; **CARB** 1.1g; **FIBER** 0g; **CHOL** 0mg; **IRON** 0.6mg; **SODIUM** 181mg; **CALC** 28mg

total time
1 hr. 16 min.

Serve cold or at room temperature with toothpicks.

DAIRY FREE

GLUTEN FREE

LOW-CARB

carbs: 16.8g ▪ **fat:** 3.7g
fiber: 1g ▪ **protein:** 4.2g

Potato Chips with Blue Cheese Dip

⅓ cup (1½ ounces) finely crumbled blue cheese
⅓ cup fat-free sour cream
2 tablespoons light mayonnaise
2 tablespoons fat-free milk

¼ teaspoon Worcestershire sauce
1 (1-pound) russet potato, thinly sliced, divided
Cooking spray
½ teaspoon salt, divided

1. Preheat oven to 400°. Place a baking sheet in oven.

2. Combine first 5 ingredients in a small bowl, stirring well. Cover and chill.

3. Place potato slices on paper towels; pat dry. Arrange half of potato slices in a single layer on preheated baking sheet coated with cooking spray. Sprinkle with ¼ teaspoon salt. Bake at 400° for 10 minutes. Turn potato slices over; bake an additional 5 minutes or until golden. Repeat procedure with remaining potatoes and remaining ¼ teaspoon salt. Serve immediately with blue cheese mixture. Serves 6 (serving size: about ½ cup chips and about 2 tablespoons dip)

CALORIES 117; **FAT** 3.7g (sat 1.6g, mono 0.6g, poly 0.1g); **PROTEIN** 4.2g; **CARB** 16.8g; **FIBER** 1g; **CHOL** 9mg; **IRON** 0.7mg; **SODIUM** 202mg; **CALC** 80mg

total time
43 min.

Bake leftover chips for 2 minutes at 450° to recrisp before eating.

GLUTEN FREE
PRE-WORKOUT

carbs: 8.4g ▪ fat: 7.5g ▪ fiber: 2.7g ▪ protein: 8.9g

Roasted Edamame

1 (16-ounce) package frozen unshelled edamame (green soybeans), thawed	¼ teaspoon ground red pepper
4 teaspoons olive oil	2 garlic cloves, minced
	½ teaspoon coarse sea salt

1. Preheat oven to 500°.

2. Pat edamame dry with paper towels. Place edamame, oil, red pepper, and garlic on a rimmed baking sheet, tossing to coat.

3. Bake at 500° for 15 minutes or until browned, stirring once. Sprinkle with salt. Serves 8 (serving size: ½ cup)

CALORIES 135; FAT 7.5g (sat 0.9g, mono 3.7g, poly 2.1g); PROTEIN 8.9g; CARB 8.4g; FIBER 2.7g; CHOL 0mg; IRON 1.6mg; SODIUM 199mg; CALC 91mg

total time
19 min.

Don't stir the edamame too frequently—it's more flavorful when it's lightly charred.

DAIRY FREE

GLUTEN FREE

HIGH PROTEIN

ENERGY SUSTAINING

carbs: 9g ■ **fat:** 2.4g
fiber: 0.9g ■ **protein:** 1g

Traditional Mexican Tomatillo Salsa

total time
13 min.

Use this versatile salsa as an accompaniment for grilled meats or scrambled eggs.

DAIRY FREE

GLUTEN FREE

6   small tomatillos
1   jalapeño pepper
1   small white onion, peeled and quartered
3   cups hot water
½   teaspoon salt

¼   cup chopped fresh cilantro
2   teaspoons fresh lime juice
60   baked blue corn tortilla chips or tortilla chip scoops

1. Discard husks and stems from tomatillos, and wash tomatillos. Remove stem from jalapeño pepper; cut pepper in half. Combine tomatillos, jalapeño halves, onion, and 3 cups hot water in a medium saucepan. Cover and bring to a boil over high heat; uncover and cook 3 minutes. Drain.

2. Place tomatillo mixture and salt in a food processor; process until finely chopped. Pour mixture into a bowl; stir in cilantro and lime juice. Serve with blue corn tortilla chips. Serves 10 (serving size: ¼ cup salsa and 6 chips)

CALORIES 61; **FAT** 2.4g (sat 0.2g, mono 0g, poly 0.1g); **PROTEIN** 1g; **CARB** 9g; **FIBER** 0.9g; **CHOL** 0mg; **IRON** 0.3mg; **SODIUM** 149mg; **CALC** 11mg

GOTTA GRAB IT!

GREAT PACKAGED SNACKS: When you're short on time, away from your kitchen, or on the go, these pre-packaged snacks are good low-calorie options.

CREAMY

■ Chobani Champions Tubes

Most yogurt sticks have added coloring and sugar to appeal to kids, but these 70-calorie sticks have nothing extra added to them. Full of probiotics and protein, they're a great portable yogurt option for any age.

■ Stonyfield 0% Fat Blueberry Greek Yogurt

Stonyfield yogurt is creamy and without the chalky taste that some Greek yogurts can have. We also love it because it comes in a variety of fruit flavors and two sizes, a 5.3-ounce cup and a 4-ounce cup.

■ Justin's Chocolate Hazelnut Butter Blend

This nut butter is made of roasted hazelnuts and almonds that are ground and blended with organic cocoa. It's made with less sugar than its competitors, making it a satisfying yet still sweet spread for apple slices, whole-wheat tortillas, or graham crackers.

■ Wholly Guacamole Classic Guacamole

When you can't make your own, this creamy, fresh-tasting guacamole is your next best choice. We love that it also comes in 100-calorie packs, which makes packing for a snack away from home easy.

CRUNCHY

■ Kellogg's Special-K Savory Herb Crackers

When you need a savory crunch, try these whole-grain crackers that provide 3 grams of fiber and protein per 120-calorie serving—more than what most crackers offer. Snack on just them, or pair with cheese for a more filling snack.

■ Snyder's of Hanover Organic Honey Whole Wheat Pretzel Sticks

These crunchy sticks have a unique flavor thanks to the whole wheat, honey, and sesame seeds used to make them. Slightly less salty than regular pretzels, they're great alone or dipped in hummus, salsa, or a nut butter.

■ Terra Sweets Medley Sea Salt Potato Chips

Made up of three different types of sweet potatoes, these chips have a slightly sweet flavor that is perfectly balanced with a dash of sea salt. No-salt-added and spiced versions are also available.

■ Kashi GoLean Crisp! Cinnamon Crumble Multigrain Cluster Cereal

Cereal isn't just for breakfast when it's this good—and this nutritious. Packed full of whole grains, protein, and fiber, these sweet crumbles add great crunch to yogurt.

SWEET

■ Yasso Raspberry Frozen Greek Yogurt Bars

Aside from the four creamy fruit flavors available, we love that each frozen treat has 6 grams of protein, provides 15% of your daily calcium, and has only 70 calories.

■ KIND Blueberry-Pecan Fruit and Nut Bar

If you're the type who prefers real food over a bar, give the KIND brand a try. Made up of only whole ingredients, we couldn't get enough of this nutritious treat that combined dried blueberries with cashews and almonds.

■ 365 Everyday Value Blueberry Blaze Trail Mix

Trail mix offers the perfect balance of sweet and salty, and this one definitely delivers. Peanuts, cashews, and almonds are mixed in with blueberries, cranberries, raisins, and white chocolate chunks.

■ Sheila G's Toffee Crunch Brownie Brittle

Imagine the crispy edges of a brownie made into a wafer-thin cookie and sprinkled with toffee chunks. What you've got is a decadent chocolate treat with a lot fewer calories and less fat than an actual brownie.

■ Special K Chocolatey Peanut Butter Protein Granola Bar

Many granola bars can look more like all-natural candy bars from a nutrient perspective, but these 110-calorie bars actually provide you with 4 grams each of protein and fiber—and taste pretty close to a candy bar, too!

SAVORY

■ Reduced Fat Cheez-It Baked Snack Crackers

There are lots of cheese-flavored crackers out there, but it's the sharp cheddar flavor in this classic cracker that made it stand out above the rest.

■ Perdue Simply Smart Lightly Breaded Chicken Chunks

We aren't big fans of processed foods, but this line is made with all-natural chicken breasts, simple ingredients, and no preservatives. With 50% less fat than conventional nuggets, these are a tasty choice when you need something more substantial.

■ Green Mountain Gringo Salsa

Fresh ingredients—ripe tomatoes, onions, and cilantro—are the secret to this chunky salsa that has a slightly sweet flavor thanks to apple cider vinegar.

■ Late July Organic Red Hot Mojo Multigrain Snack Chips

Dense and hearty, these multigrain tortilla chips have some heat that pairs perfectly with guacamole. If you're not sure about the spice, try the Sea Salt or SubLime flavor.

■ Sabra Roasted Pine Nut Hummus

We love all the flavors of rich, creamy, and fresh-tasting Sabra hummus. But the roasted pine nuts add an extra depth of flavor.

■ Emerald Sea Salt & Pepper Cashews

Pepper adds a surprising but not-too-spicy kick to these roasted nuts. The nuts' protein and heart-healthy fats combined with their simple seasonings make them a great option for when you're looking for a filling savory snack.

MAKE IT A MEAL!

MENU NUTRITIONAL INFORMATION

CREAMY

Curried Yogurt Dip, *page 21*
CALORIES 350; FAT 23.6g (sat 1.5g); PROTEIN 18.9g;
CARB 40.6g; FIBER 3.6g; SODIUM 594mg

Feta-Mint Dip, *page 23*
CALORIES 314; FAT 16.0g (sat 4.8g); PROTEIN 14.4g;
CARB 30g; FIBER 4.6g; SODIUM 552mg

Fresh Herb Dip, *page 27*
CALORIES 349; FAT 13.5g (sat 5.8g); PROTEIN 34.0g;
CARB 23.6g; FIBER 3.8g; SODIUM 556mg

Lemon, Mint, and White Bean Dip,
page 37
CALORIES 371; FAT 11.8g (sat 3.5g); PROTEIN 12.5g;
CARB 55.2g; FIBER 8.9g; SODIUM 576mg

Lemon-Spinach Dip with Walnuts,
page 49
CALORIES 377; FAT 20.7g (sat 2.9g); PROTEIN 18.5g;
CARB 31.6g; FIBER 6.5g; SODIUM 273mg;

Roasted Garlic-Cream Cheese Balls,
page 29
CALORIES 350; FAT 13.3g (sat 6.3g); PROTEIN 8.8g;
CARB 49.7g; FIBER 6.5g;
SODIUM 664mg

Tomato-Avocado Dip, *page 53*
CALORIES 475; FAT 12.2g (sat 4.0g); PROTEIN 16.1g;
CARB 75.8g; FIBER 12.0g; SODIUM 677mg

Vanilla-Berry Smoothies, *page 11*
CALORIES 427; FAT 19.3g (sat 3.8g); PROTEIN 19.7g;
CARB 50.8g; FIBER 4.7g; SODIUM 339mg

CRUNCHY

Almond-Apricot Granola, *page 57*
CALORIES 379; FAT 7.6g (sat 0.7g); PROTEIN 15.1g;
CARB 66.1g; FIBER 12.4g; SODIUM 383mg

Cheddar-Apple Cracker Bites, *page 59*
CALORIES 361; FAT 8.3g (sat 4.2g); PROTEIN 14.5g;
CARB 60g; FIBER 4.9g; SODIUM 484mg

**Crostini with Sun-Dried Tomato-Olive
Tapenade,** *page 71*
CALORIES 420; FAT 26.1g (sat 4.7g); PROTEIN 33.0g;
CARB 13.7g; FIBER 3.3g; SODIUM 537mg

Curried Chutney-Stuffed Celery,
page 73
CALORIES 365; FAT 6.6g (sat 2.0g); PROTEIN 24.0g;
CARB 58.1g; FIBER 12.0g; SODIUM 844mg

Glazed Honey Nuts, *page 103*
CALORIES 324; FAT 18.9g (sat 1.6g); PROTEIN 10.8g;
CARB 30.7g; FIBER 5.5g; SODIUM 315mg

Peanut-Raisin Snack Mix, *page 85*
CALORIES 411; FAT 11.7g (sat 3.7g); PROTEIN 12.9g;
CARB 69.1g; FIBER 6.9g; SODIUM 233mg

Spiced Sweet Potato Chips, *page 91*
CALORIES 324; FAT 7.0g (sat 2.5g); PROTEIN 23.8g;
CARB 44.4g; FIBER 7.6g; SODIUM 896mg

Strawberry-Cereal Snack Bars,
page 93
CALORIES 313; FAT 3.3g (sat 1.7g); PROTEIN 13.6g;
CARB 60.9g; FIBER 7.2g; SODIUM 169mg;

Sweet and Spicy Pumpkinseeds,
page 99
CALORIES 403; FAT 22.0g (sat 7.9g); PROTEIN 38.2g;
CARB 13.3g; FIBER 3.3g; SODIUM 553mg

SWEET

Caramel-Apple Crunch Bars, *page 151*
CALORIES 351; **FAT** 11.9g (sat 3.1g); **PROTEIN** 11.3g;
CARB 52.4g; **FIBER** 6.9g **SODIUM** 706mg

**Chocolate-Granola-Yogurt Crunch
Parfaits,** *page 113*
CALORIES 468; **FAT** 16.1g (sat 4.6g); **PROTEIN** 15.0g;
CARB 68.8g; **FIBER** 3.5g **SODIUM** 671mg

Granola Cookie Wedges, *page 129*
CALORIES 503; **FAT** 7.0g (sat 1.5g); **PROTEIN** 25.3g;
CARB 86.2g; **FIBER** 4.5g **SODIUM** 347mg

Peaches-and-Cream Ice Pops, *page 141*
CALORIES 397; **FAT** 14.2g (sat 6.1g); **PROTEIN** 35.3g;
CARB 38.6g; **FIBER** 6.6g **SODIUM** 140mg

Peanut Butter–Banana Quesadilla,
page 143
CALORIES 432; **FAT** 15.6g (sat 2.6g); **PROTEIN** 13.8g;
CARB 65g; **FIBER** 9.3g; **SODIUM** 414mg

Peanutty Granola Bars, *page 153*
CALORIES 389; **FAT** 15.7g (sat 3.8g); **PROTEIN** 17.1g;
CARB 49.2g; **FIBER** 4.8g; **SODIUM** 102mg

SAVORY

Barbecue Pizza Bites, *page 171*
CALORIES 340; **FAT** 12.0g (sat 3.6g); **PROTEIN** 18.9g;
CARB 40.6g; **FIBER** 3.6g; **SODIUM** 594mg

**Chicken Nuggets with Mustard
Sauce,** *page 175*
CALORIES 355; **FAT** 4.6g (sat 0.8g); **PROTEIN** 26.9g;
CARB 52.5g; **FIBER** 5.1g; **SODIUM** 363mg

Fig-Goat Cheese Phyllo Bites, *page 181*
CALORIES 304; **FAT** 13.6g (sat 4.2g); **PROTEIN** 10.2g;
CARB 36.6g; **FIBER** 4.8g; **SODIUM** 436mg

Hot Bean-and-Cheese Dip, *page 191*
CALORIES 364; **FAT** 16.1g (sat 4.2g); **PROTEIN** 11.9g;
CARB 41.3g; **FIBER** 7.2g; **SODIUM** 550mg

Mini Cheddar Potato Skins, *page 197*
CALORIES 379; **FAT** 11.8g (sat 5.7g); **PROTEIN** 32.7g;
CARB 37.4g; **FIBER** 7.6g; **SODIUM** 296mg

Pear and Swiss Triangles, *page 203*
CALORIES 389; **FAT** 8.1g (sat 4.6g); **PROTEIN** 18.9g;
CARB 64.7g; **FIBER** 8.7g; **CHOL** 45mg; **IRON** 4.4mg;
SODIUM 422mg; **CALC** 637mg

nutritional information

How to Use It and Why

Glance at the end of any *Cooking Light* recipe, and you'll see how committed we are to helping you make the best of today's light cooking. With chefs, registered dietitians, home economists, and a computer system that analyzes every ingredient we use, *Cooking Light* gives you authoritative dietary detail like no other magazine. We go to such lengths so you can see how our recipes fit into your healthful eating plan. If you're trying to lose weight, the calorie and fat figures will probably help most. But if you're keeping a close eye on the sodium, cholesterol, and saturated fat in your diet, we provide those numbers, too.

And because many women don't get enough iron or calcium, we can help there, as well. Finally, there's a fiber analysis for those of us who don't get enough roughage.

Here's a helpful guide to put our nutritional analysis numbers into perspective. Remember, one size doesn't fit all, so take your lifestyle, age, and circumstances into consideration when determining your nutrition needs. For example, pregnant or breast-feeding women need more protein, calories, and calcium. Women older than 50 need 1,200mg of calcium daily, 200mg more than the amount recommended for younger women.

In Our Nutritional Analysis, We Use These Abbreviations

sat	saturated fat	CARB	carbohydrates	g	gram
mono	monounsaturated fat	CHOL	cholesterol	mg	milligram
poly	polyunsaturated fat	CALC	calcium		

Daily Nutrition Guide

	Women ages 25 to 50	Women over 50	Men ages 24 to 50	Men over 50
Calories	2,000	2,000 or less	2,700	2,500
Protein	50g	50g or less	63g	60g
Fat	65g or less	65g or less	88g or less	83g or less
Saturated Fat	20g or less	20g or less	27g or less	25g or less
Carbohydrates	304g	304g	410g	375g
Fiber	25g to 35g	25g to 35g	25g to 35g	25g to 35g
Cholesterol	300mg or less	300mg or less	300mg or less	300mg or less
Iron	18mg	8mg	8mg	8mg
Sodium	2,300mg or less	1,500mg or less	2,300mg or less	1,500mg or less
Calcium	1,000mg	1,200mg	1,000mg	1,000mg

The nutritional values used in our calculations either come from The Food Processor, Version 10.4 (ESHA Research), or are provided by food manufacturers.

metric equivalents

The information in the following charts is provided to help cooks outside the United States successfully use the recipes in this book. All equivalents are approximate.

Cooking/Oven Temperatures

Fahrenheit	Celsius	Gas Mark	
Freeze Water	32° F	0° C	
Room Temp.	68° F	20° C	
Boil Water	212° F	100° C	
Bake	325° F	160° C	3
	350° F	180° C	4
	375° F	190° C	5
	400° F	200° C	6
	425° F	220° C	7
	450° F	230° C	8
Broil			Grill

Liquid Ingredients by Volume

¼ tsp	=					1 ml
½ tsp	=					2 ml
1 tsp	=					5 ml
3 tsp	=	1 Tbsp	=	½ fl oz	=	15 ml
2 Tbsp	=	⅛ cup	=	1 fl oz	=	30 ml
4 Tbsp	=	¼ cup	=	2 fl oz	=	60 ml
5⅓ Tbsp	=	⅓ cup	=	3 fl oz	=	80 ml
8 Tbsp	=	½ cup	=	4 fl oz	=	120 ml
10⅔ Tbsp	=	⅔ cup	=	5 fl oz	=	160 ml
12 Tbsp	=	¾ cup	=	6 fl oz	=	180 ml
16 Tbsp	=	1 cup	=	8 fl oz	=	240 ml
1 pt	=	2 cups	=	16 fl oz	=	480 ml
1 qt	=	4 cups	=	32 fl oz	=	960 ml
				33 fl oz	= 1000 ml	= 1 l

Dry Ingredients by Weight

(To convert ounces to grams, multiply the number of ounces by 30.)

1 oz	=	¹⁄₁₆ lb	=	30 g
4 oz	=	¼ lb	=	120 g
8 oz	=	½ lb	=	240 g
12 oz	=	¾ lb	=	360 g
16 oz	=	1 lb	=	480 g

Length

(To convert inches to centimeters, multiply the number of inches by 2.5.)

1 in	=			2.5 cm	
6 in	=	½ ft	=	15 cm	
12 in	=	1 ft	=	30 cm	
36 in	=	3 ft	= 1 yd	90 cm	
40 in	=			100 cm	= 1 m

Equivalents for Different Types of Ingredients

Standard Cup	Fine Powder (ex. flour)	Grain (ex. rice)	Granular (ex. sugar)	Liquid Solids (ex. butter)	Liquid (ex. milk)
1	140 g	150 g	190 g	200 g	240 ml
¾	105 g	113 g	143 g	150 g	180 ml
⅔	93 g	100 g	125 g	133 g	160 ml
½	70 g	75 g	95 g	100 g	120 ml
⅓	47 g	50 g	63 g	67 g	80 ml
¼	35 g	38 g	48 g	50 g	60 ml
⅛	18 g	19 g	24 g	25 g	30 ml

index

©2014 by Time Home Entertainment Inc.
135 West 50th Street, New York, NY 10020

ISBN-13: 978-0-8487-0427-8
ISBN-10: 0-8487-0427-4
Library of Congress Control Number: 2013954813
Printed in the United States of America
First Printing 2014

Oxmoor House
Vice President, Brand Publishing: Laura Sappington
Editorial Director: Leah McLaughlin
Creative Director: Felicity Keane
Art Director: Christopher Rhoads
Brand Manager: Michelle Turner Aycock
Senior Editor: Andrea C. Kirkland, MS, RD
Managing Editor: Elizabeth Tyler Austin
Assistant Managing Editor: Jeanne de Lathouder

SNacKTaSTiC!

Editor: Shaun Chavis
Senior Designer: J. Shay McNamee
Project Editor: Lacie Pinyan
Assistant Designer: Allison Sperando Potter
Junior Designer: Maribeth Jones
Executive Food Director: Grace Parisi
Assistant Test Kitchen Manager: Alyson Moreland Haynes
Recipe Developers and Testers: Wendy Ball, RD; Tamara Goldis, RD; Stefanie Maloney; Callie Nash; Karen Rankin; Leah Van Deren
Food Stylists: Victoria E. Cox, Margaret Monroe Dickey, Catherine Crowell Steele
Photography Director: Jim Bathie
Senior Photographer: Hélène Dujardin
Senior Photo Stylist: Kay E. Clarke
Photo Stylist: Mindi Shapiro Levine
Assistant Photo Stylist: Mary Louise Menendez
Production Manager: Tamara Nall Wilder
Assistant Production Manager: Diane Rose Keener

Contributors
Recipe Developer and Tester: Jan Smith
Compositor: Frances Higginbotham
Illustrator: Serge Bloch
Copy Editors: Jacqueline Giovanelli, *Marrathon Production Services*
Nutrition Analysis: Carolyn Land Williams, PhD, RD
Indexer: *Marrathon Production Services*
Fellows: Ali Carruba, Elizabeth Laseter, Amy Pinney, Madison Taylor Pozzo, Deanna Sakal, April Smitherman, Megan Thompson, Tonya West
Food Stylists: Erica Hopper
Photo Stylists: Mary Clayton Carl, Lydia DeGaris Pursell, Leslie Simpson

Cooking Light®
Editor: Scott Mowbray
Creative Director: Dimity Jones
Executive Managing Editor: Phillip Rhodes
Executive Editor, Food: Ann Taylor Pittman
Executive Editor, Digital: Allison Long Lowery
Senior Food Editor: Timothy Q. Cebula
Senior Editor: Cindy Hatcher
Assistant Editor, Nutrition: Sidney Fry, MS, RD
Assistant Editors: Kimberly Holland, Hannah Klinger
Test Kitchen Manager: Tiffany Vickers Davis
Recipe Testers and Developers: Robin Bashinsky, Adam Hickman, Deb Wise
Art Directors: Rachel Cardina Lasserre, Sheri Wilson
Senior Designer: Anna Bird
Designer: Hagen Stegall
Assistant Designer: Nicole Gerrity
Assistant Photo Editor: Amy Delaune
Senior Photographer: Randy Mayor
Chief Food Stylist: Kellie Gerber Kelley
Food Styling Assistant: Blakeslee Giles
Production Director: Liz Rhoades
Production Editor: Hazel R. Eddins
Production Coordinator: Caitlin Murphree Miller
Assistant Copy Chief: Susan Roberts
CookingLight.com Editor: Mallory Daugherty Brasseale
CookingLight.com Assistant Editor/Producer: Michelle Klug

Time Home Entertainment Inc.
President and Publisher: Jim Childs
Vice President, Brand & Digital Strategy: Steven Sandonato
Vice President, Finance: Vandana Patel
Executive Director, Marketing Services: Carol Pittard
Executive Director, Retail & Special Sales: Tom Mifsud
Director, Bookazine Development & Marketing: Laura Adam
Executive Publishing Director: Joy Butts
Associate Publishing Director: Megan Pearlman
Associate General Counsel: Helen Wan